B.C. Provincial Police Stories

by CECIL CLARK

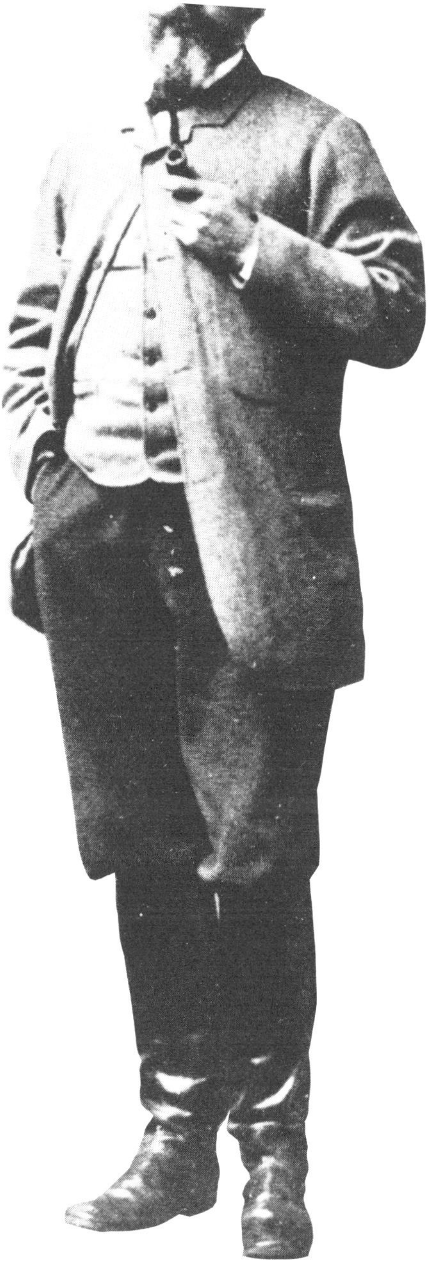

In 1858 Matthew Baillie Begbie became the first judge in the Crown Colony of British Columbia. Called by one miner " . . . the damndest man that ever came over the Cariboo Road," he became Chief Justice of British Columbia and was knighted for his outstanding role in helping maintain law and order in a frontier land.

THE COVER

The B.C. Provincial Police lock-up at Soda Creek was one of nearly 100 throughout the province which provided living quarters for a constable and cells for miscreants. At about $400 each, they were a bargain. The one at Soda Creek has survived almost a century and is in remarkably good condition. It should be preserved as a memorial to the men of the B.C. Provincial Police.

PHOTO CREDITS

B.C. Provincial Archives, all photos not otherwise credited; Clark, Cecil 4, 6-7; Glenbow Archives, 105; Heritage House, 19, front and back covers, inside front cover, top; Public Archives Canada, 17 C61937, 34-35 16080; Ramsey, Bruce, 39; RCMP, 104; Tourism B.C., inside front cover, lower, inside back cover, marine scene.

CANADIAN CATALOGUING IN PUBLICATION DATA

Clark, Cecil, 1899-
    B.C. Provincial Police stories

ISBN 0-919214-74-6

1. Crime and criminals — British Columbia — History. I. Title.
HV6809.B7C53 1986   364.1'09711   C86-091097-0

HERITAGE HOUSE PUBLISHING COMPANY LTD.
Box 1228, Station A, Surrey. B.C. V3S 2B3

Printed in Canada.

PRINTING HISTORY
First Edition — 1988
Second Printing — 1990
Third Printing — 1993

CONTENTS

The author when he was Inspector Cecil Clark, Commanding "E" Division of the B.C. Provincial Police at Vancouver. He knew many of the men about whom he writes and the cases on which they worked.

THE AUTHOR

Cecil (Nobby) Clark was 17 when he enlisted as a constable in the B.C. Provincial Police. He served for thirty-five years — more than one-third of the force's ninety-two-year history — rising to the rank of Deputy Commissioner. In so doing he maintained a tradition of which the force was very proud — all senior officers, with the exception of the first appointment in 1858 when the force was born, rose from the ranks.

After Clark's retirement in 1950 his active service didn't end, it simply changed direction. Since the force had only about 100 members when he joined he knew many of the pioneer policemen and worked on the later cases, interrogating rum-runners, thieves, and murderers. He became the force's unofficial historian, but instead of writing a history which few people would read, Clark presented a popular cross-section of the force's hundreds of cases.

To complement his personal knowledge, he spent years researching in the Provincial Archives at Victoria, various libraries and official police records. The dry evidence he uncovered he transformed into tales of adventure and suspense that take the reader on a journey from the frontier British Columbia of the 1860s to the 1950s when the B.C. Provincial Police was absorbed by the Royal Canadian Mounted Police.

DEDICATION

This book is a memorial to the men of the B.C. Provincial Police who in 1858 with a quiet sense of duty began to curb the lawless.

For decades horses were the main means of travel with weeks in the saddle not uncommon, although horses were often replaced by canoes and boats in summer, snowshoes and dog teams in winter. Other policemen were adept with tiller and mainsail as they

DEDICATED ON DECEMBER 1, 1973. THIS PLAQUE HONOURS THE WORK OF THE FORMER BRITISH COLUMBIA PROVINCIAL POLICE.

FORMED ON NOVEMBER 19, 1858. THIS, THE OLDEST TERRITORIAL POLICE FORCE IN CANADA, SERVED THE PEOPLE OF BRITISH COLUMBIA WITH HONOUR, PRIDE AND UNSELFISH DUTY UNTIL AUGUST 14, 1950.

THE "B. C. POLICE." AS IT WAS COMMONLY AND RESPECTFULLY KNOWN, DEMONSTRATED ON LAND, SEA AND IN THE AIR. THE HIGHEST QUALITIES DEMANDED OF ANY POLICE FORCE IN THE WORLD.

B. C. CENTENNIAL COMMITTEE
B. C. PROVINCIAL POLICE
VETERAN'S ASSOCIATION

Plaque at the Provincial Museum-Archives complex at Victoria.

patrolled B.C.'s 5,000-mile (8,000-km) coastline. Then in the 1890s came launches with open naptha engines which were gradually replaced by a fleet of diesel-powered cruisers. Finally arrived the air age and some officers piloted planes.

These far-ranging police officers saw not only the coming of the telegraph, the telephone and electric light but also were on duty when the four-horse stagecoach gave way to the train, the automobile and the airplane. They readily embraced anything new that would make them more efficient and were proud that their experiments enabled them to establish the first city-to-city short wave police radio communication system in North America.

Whether assisting victims of fire or flood, escorting fugitives from foreign countries, or merely performing the daily routine of urban duty, these British Columbia policemen did it with pride born of a sense of history. Many died in the performance of their duty, expecting nothing more than that they be remembered.

There is no question that they were held high in public esteem in their ninety-two-year history. Similarly, when absorbed into the Royal Canadian Mounted Police in the summer of 1950, they were regarded by the Federal Force as a rather exceptional corps.

To the British Columbia Provincial Police — the living and the dead — the men who served British Columbia so well, this book is dedicated.

INTRODUCTION

Whether or not television encourages violence is a frequently debated question, but there is no debate on another aspect of TV programming — the medium has grown wealthy from programs which feature the Old West and its ever present gunfire. At the Canadian border, however, the six-shooter Western saga never had a chance to incubate.

While it is true that British Columbia, born of the quest for furs and gold, had the usual early-day frontier society, it was a frontier scene with a difference. It had law and order.

Kamloops Detachment of the B.C. Police in the early 1940s. Sitting at left is Staff Sergeant Andy Fairbairn who helped solve the Hudock murder. (See page 48.)

Murders were committed, of course, but the culprits were usually apprehended. Then they were swiftly tried and, if found guilty, usually hanged. The first judge on the Mainland of B.C. (then called the Colony of British Columbia) was Matthew Baillie Begbie. He was selected because Sir Edward Bulwer Lytton, Colonial Secretary in London, wanted a young, athletic man who in Lytton's own words: "Must be a man who could, if necessary, truss a murderer up and hang him from the nearest tree."

While Begbie didn't hang anybody himself, he became the terror of evil doers, a legend who established a formidable reputation. As noted in Heritage House book, *Wagon Road North — Historical Photos from 1863 of the Cariboo Gold Rush:*

"He always carried his robes and wore them wherever he held court, whether it be a tent, store, saloon, or cabin. He was called a hanging judge, but he never hanged a man the jury didn't convict, and hanging was the only legal penalty for murder. His drumhead justice was the law that

American miners could understand; his fearlessness won the respect of all. He was willing to fight with fists or with lawbooks, and never relented. At Clinton he once sentenced a man and later in his hotel room heard the fellow's companions plotting to shoot him. The Judge listened for awhile, then emptied his chamber pot over them.

"Dr. Cheadle passed the Judge near Clinton on the Cariboo Wagon Road in 1863 and wrote: 'Passed Judge Begbie on horseback. Everybody praises his just severity as the salvation of Cariboo and terror of rowdies.'

"One miner summed him up thus: 'Begbie was the biggest man, the smartest man, the best looking man, and the damndest man that ever came over the Cariboo Road.'

"Judge Begbie died at Victoria in 1894, Chief Justice of British Columbia. He had helped guide the Province through an era when he and a few policemen were the only difference between justice by might and justice by right."

Another lawman who gained a reputation for toughness was Peter O'Reilly. In April 1859 he was appointed a stipendiary magistrate and in the early 1860s was sent to Wild Horse Creek in what is today the East Kootenay, scene of a gold rush that attracted several thousand miners, mostly from the U.S. Here O'Reilly delivered an address that has become a legend.

Since there was no stenographer to record his words there are many versions of what he said. Possibly the most accurate is in a book called *Sport and Life in the Hunting Grounds of Western America and British Columbia*. It was written by W. A. Baillie-Grohman, a sportsman-developer who arrived in the East Kootenay in 1882. According to Baillie-Grohman, when O'Reilly arrived at Wild Horse he addressed a group of miners in front of "the single-roomed cabin which he had turned into a temporary courthouse . . . and made a famous speech which is still remembered throughout the mining camps. . . . Standing near the pole from which floated the Union Jack . . . he said: 'Boys, I am here to keep order and to administer the law. Those who don't want law and order can git, but those who stay with the camp, remember on what side of the line the camp is; for, boys, if there is shooting in Kootenay there will be hanging in Kootenay."

Only one flurry of gun play erupted at Wild Horse, promptly settled in judicial style by 27-year-old Magistrate and Constable John C. Haynes. A month or two later when Colonial Secretary Arthur N. Birch visited the scene after twenty-four days in the saddle from Hope on the Fraser River he reported:

"I found the British Columbia mining laws in full force, all customs duties paid, no pistols to be seen and everything as quiet and orderly as it could possibly be in the most civilized district of the colony . . . much to the surprise and admiration of many who remembered the early days of the state of California."

The measure of the miner's regard for the four policemen ultimately stationed at Wild Horse was demonstrated when Constable John Lawson was killed there by a horse thief named Charlie "One Ear" Brown who fled across the U.S. border to apparent safety. A quartet of miners promptly pursued One Ear to the border but didn't bother with the for-

The B.C. Police pioneered short-wave radio communication in North America. At top is Inspector Fernie's car at Kamloops in 1928 with a radio antenna on the roof, part of an experiment with two-way radio in vehicles.

At right is the first radio equipment installed in Nelson in 1929.

The bottom photo shows police and their patrol cars in the 1930s. Even then, however, over much of B.C. the main method of patrolling was by dog team and on snowshoes in winter, by horses or boats in summer.

mality of waiting for customs and immigration. They kept on going, caught him, and shot him. (See page 116.)

During the almost century-long era that the B.C. Provincial Police were the front line of law and order they were always few in number. Even by 1900 there were only 100 to police an area some 50 per cent larger than France. They nevertheless maintained the peace, and well, even though they occasionally bent the rules. One example is related in the chapter "Murder on the Trail of '98."

The work of these pioneer policemen is the theme of the chapters which follow. They functioned in a land once described by Canada's famed humorist Stephen Leacock as "an empire in itself" — albeit a rugged empire amidst a sea of snowcapped peaks. Some have dubbed it the land of exaggeration. Extremes is perhaps the better word, considering that among its offshore islands tides can race up to 16 knots, in mountain passes wintertime snowfall can be 65 feet, (19 m) and temperatures range from 109 degrees in the shade to 72 below zero F. (42.8 to -56.7 C).

All of which emphasizes that the province's pioneer policemen had many discomforting days in the saddle, on snowshoes along lonely bush trails, in canoes and riverboats, and on the wind-aroused waters of B.C.'s multi-thousand-mile coastline. There are many recorded instances of them bringing their prisoners by horse and canoe 1,000 miles (1,600 km) to a courtroom.

As far back as January 1863, Chief Justice Matthew Baillie Begbie, in a plea to Governor James Douglas for increased police pay, had this to say of them:

"The fact is that most of the constables in the upper country are men who have hitherto filled superior stations in life; some of them having even held field officers' commissions in Her Majesty's army and most of them are provided with some small means of their own. But for this, it is an arithmetical certainty that they could not exist without running into debt, which would very much interfere with their utility. They are kept upright in their present position by the habit of discipline, by a sense of honor and by the hope of speedy promotion. . . ."

With law enforcement in such hands and even though in 1858 over 30,000 heavily armed miners from the U.S. stampeded to the Fraser River, there was remarkably little lawlessness — despite the fact that miners outnumbered policemen by over one thousand to one. Hubert Howe Bancroft, the Pacific Northwest's foremost historian, observed: "Never in the pacification and settlement of any section of America have there been so few disturbances, so few crimes against life and property."

Perhaps it is needless for me to note that these tales of law enforcement are as factually correct as years of research can make them. But as they span a century, changes in jurisdiction and rank may occasionally be puzzling. For clearer understanding a little background information is perhaps appropriate.

In 1858 the sudden influx of tens of thousands of gold seekers into the rocky canyons of the Fraser River transformed the fur-trading character of Britain's Pacific Coast colony into a copy of the 1849 stampede to California.

To organize a constabulary in the newly proclaimed colony, Britain's Colonial Secretary despatched 43-year-old Sub-Inspector Chartres Brew of the Royal Irish Constabulary. Immediately on Brew's arrival, Governor Douglas appointed him Chief Inspector of Police. The date was November 19, 1858, and the site of the swearing-in ceremony Fort Langley on the Fraser River just east of today's Vancouver.

Brew's handful of locally recruited policemen soon extended their activities to a new gold strike on Williams Creek in the Cariboo Country. Later they were on hand when a fresh bonanza was uncovered at Wild Horse Creek in the southeast corner of the colony. Thereafter, whenever a miner found gold, a policeman was soon at his elbow.

In this fashion the force penetrated into the wilds of the Omineca and, finally, the far distant Cassiar and Stikine. By this time British Columbia had become a Canadian province and Brew's colonial police now known as provincial police. Fifteen years later in 1874, the North-West Mounted Police made their red serge the symbol of law and order on Canada's central plains. The B.C. Police, however, had predated the Mounties by sixteen years. In the course of time the force was divided into fourteen districts, each with a Chief Constable in charge. In each district Constables were in charge of detachments.

The system lasted sixty-six years, then in 1924 semi-military ranks and uniforms were introduced. Instead of keeping in contact with a multitude of districts the Superintendent (now ranked as Commissioner) communicated only with Inspectors commanding five divisions.

Finally, in 1950, in the force's ninety-second year, an agreement between B.C. and the Federal government was ratified whereby the Royal Canadian Mounted Police assumed responsibility for law enforcement. The bulk of the B.C. Police was absorbed into the Mounted Police.

Though nearly forty years have elapsed since their familiar khaki and green uniforms disappeared, ex-British Columbia policemen continue to gather at an annual re-union dinner, all proud of having once been associated with North America's oldest territorial constabulary.

Finally, I might add that in assembling material for this book, though many of the latter-day stories come from personal first-hand knowledge, those stemming from an earlier period required a good deal of research in British Columbia's Archives. I would indeed be remiss, therefore, if I failed to acknowledge my deep sense of gratitude to the late Provincial Archivist Willard Ireland and the very capable Archives staff.

I also wish to thank the original publisher of these articles, "The Islander," Sunday magazine of the Victoria *Daily Colonist*, for permission to reprint them, and also Gray's Publishing Ltd. of Sidney, B.C., who presented many of them in an out-of-print, hard-cover book, *Tales of the British Columbia Provincial Police*.

Cecil Clark
Victoria, B.C.

The Evidence of the Gold Nugget Stick Pin

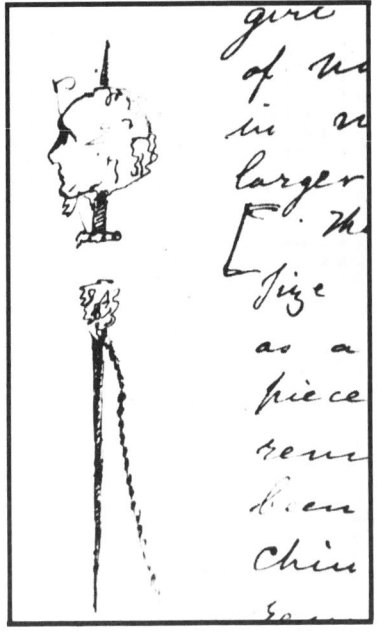

The sketch of the stick pin which Judge Begbie made in his bench book during the 1867 trial.

The gambler was confident that he had committed a perfect murder. He perhaps would have — except for Barkerville's gold rush barber, Wellington D. Moses.

On a sultry afternoon in early August 1866, Wellington Delaney Moses, Barkerville's Negro barber, beckoned the next customer to the chair. He was James Barry, one of the town gamblers, a tall hard-faced Texan who slung his broad-rimmed felt hat on a peg and, with a curt nod of recognition, took his seat. Although they had met before, Barry, the southerner, was holding fast to his ingrained ideas about color.

As Moses slipped the white sheet under Barry's chin, he suddenly paused. A gold nugget stick pin on the gambler's black string tie held the barber's attention. Although the pause was only for a second, it started a sequence that twelve months later ended with Barry's death — at the end of a rope.

It was late when Moses finally closed and retired to his bedroom behind the barber shop. On this night, like many others, he found it hard to sleep, mainly because on the other side of the pitch pine wall was Ross and Bur-

Barkerville in 1868 a few days before it was destroyed in a fire. Somewhere among the buildings is Moses' Barber Shop.

dick's Dance Hall and Saloon. Long after midnight, through the rough siding, the hoot and stamp of miners and girls and the frenzied sawing of fiddlers invaded the room. Moses lay awake thinking of Barry's nugget pin. It worried him because in a vague sort of way he knew he'd seen it before. And then he remembered. The nugget pin belonged to Charles Blessing. He was sure of it. There couldn't be another like it.

Moses' association with Blessing had its origin in 1858 when gold was discovered on the bars of the Fraser River. Upwards of 30,000 men stampeded northward from California and elsewhere, among them Wellington Moses. But instead of heading for the gravel bars of the Fraser, Moses started Victoria's first barber shop. He also offered customers the luxury of a bath, despite the fact that water was a scarce commodity which was peddled from a horse-drawn barrel at forty buckets for a dollar.

The subsequent Cariboo mining boom of the middle 1860s that made Barkerville the biggest town in the Canadian west pulled Moses in that direction. He opened a shop in Barkerville that must have been profitable since he followed the custom of the affluent by wintering in Victoria when the Cariboo's long winter closed down mining. It was in the spring of 1866 that Moses, on the journey back to Barkerville, met Charles Morgan Blessing at Yale. As they were both heading in the same direction, they decided to travel together — "chummies," in the language of the day.

Blessing was 30, scion of a wealthy New England family. He had followed the wanderlust for gold, first to California, then British Columbia. Despite rubbing shoulders with the roughest of men, he had retained his gentlemanly manner. As a Northerner, he had more liberal views toward color, and apparently found in Moses an independence of mind that few New Englanders had encountered.

The two travelled the Cariboo Road in one of Barnard's six-horse stages, up through the sagebrush country to Soda Creek from where they caught the sternwheeler to Quesnel, arriving about 7 pm, May 28. Since accommodation was scarce, they went to bed "in the custom of the country" which meant rolling out their blankets on Brown and Gillis' Saloon floor in the company of other tired travellers. At the end of the room the bar kept open, the sleepers oblivious to the noise.

The next afternoon Moses and his friend fell in with James Barry, or rather Barry seemed to fall into their company. Slick and debonair, it was plain to them that if Barry toiled with his hands it wasn't in a mine. To their questions he conceded he had a natural bent for the intricacies of any card game involving money. Blessing suggested they adjourn for a drink. It was then that gambler Barry admitted that his card sense had lately gone awry. He was broke.

Blessing opened his wallet at the bar and drew out a $20 Bank of British Columbia note, upon which Moses gave him the quiet tip to avoid spending too much.

Said Blessing, with a grin, "I've got a few more of these before I'm broke." Neither apparently noticed the look of sudden interest in Barry's face.

After a few drinks it was agreed that Blessing and Barry would start the next morning along the trail for Barkerville since Moses had decided to stay in Quesnel to find a man who owed him some money. Barry suggested that in order to avoid the crowded sleeping quarters in the saloon, he and Blessing bunk down in a nearby vacant shack. With a "goodnight" to Moses they moved off into the dark. Next morning Moses sought out the shack but they were gone. An Indian camped nearby said he'd seen them fold their blankets and head for the Barkerville wagon road about daylight.

When Moses arrived in Barkerville and looked around for Blessing, he ran into Barry coming out of Jimmy Loring's Saloon. The gambler would have passed the barber had not Moses grabbed him by the arm to enquire about his friend.

"Oh, that fellow," drawled Barry, as if he had a hard time recalling him. "He wasn't much good on the trail. Got sore feet or something and quit. I think he went back to Quesnel."

Weeks passed, and as Moses plied his scissors and razor he occasionally thought of Blessing and the nugget pin he had shown him on the way up from Yale. Often he asked a newly arrived miner whether he had heard of him. But nobody had.

Barry, meantime, was here and there around Barkerville, Richfield and Camerontown. Though separately named they were practically one community linked by a long main street, distinguished not only for the size of potholes but for the number and variety of saloons, most with dance hall and gambling facilities.

At night, in bedlam under the glare of naphtha lamps, each saloon proprietor did his best to separate the miners from their pokes. Added attractions were the "hurdies," buxom girls, recruited mainly from Germany and Holland, who invariably wore a red blouse, hoop skirt and around their heads a red bandana, the bow on top. Their "day" started about eight in the evening, when for a dollar a dance they were whirled off their feet by exuberant miners to the jigging tempo of fiddle and concertina. After each dance (about one whirl around the floor) the girls led their bearded and booted partners to the bar, where they got a commission on the drinks.

Gambler Barry was at home in this scene and his smooth approach made him a favorite with most of the girls. When he wasn't manipulating cards or dice, he was rated Don Juan of the dance halls — a reputation that required an occasional visit to the barber.

When Moses remembered where he'd last seen the nugget pin, he realized that Barry might have had something to do with Blessing's non-appearance in Barkerville. Moses knew that Blessing thought a lot of the pin and he certainly would not have sold or given it away to a chance acquaintance of Barry's type. Besides, he didn't have to sell it, he had money.

Money! It increased Moses' feeling that something had happened to his friend. True, Barry was adept at coming out on the right side of a card or dice game, or collecting a slice of the earnings of some infatuated "hurdy." But how much money did he have when he arrived?

The next day Moses locked his shop and began some discreet enquiries. Finally, he got the information he wanted. From Sam Wilcox, boardinghouse keeper, he learned that when Barry arrived in Barkerville in early June he took a room at Wilcox's for $12 a week. Asked to pay in advance,

the man who was broke at Quesnel on May 29 had a $20 Bank of British Columbia bill on June 2. Back in his barbershop bedroom Moses was undecided whether to tell his story to the B.C. Police at Richfield about one mile away. Then he thought better of it. After all, it was only suspicion.

A few weeks passed, then in late September Moses was cutting the hair of Bill Fraser, one of the men who had landed in Victoria in 1858. He knew a lot of Moses' early-day Victoria customers and Moses asked him if he'd ever run across a gambler called Barry.

"That character! Why? You a friend of his?"

Moses intimated he had an interest in Barry's background. By coincidence, Fraser once had travelled up from New Westminster with Barry. On the road he had concluded from remarks Barry made that the tall Texan had seen the interior of more than one jail. He also seemed to know the inside story of a few recent robberies. When Fraser asked him how, Barry admitted he'd heard about them from "a fellow who was in the chain gang with me at New Westminster."

Fraser noted that Barry always wore a Colt six-gun and cartridge belt. The miner was interested in the gun because he had a friend in New Westminster who had just lost one. In fact the friend had supplied Fraser with its serial number in case he ran across it. Once or twice on the trip Fraser tried to steer the conversation to guns, hoping to get a chance to

The rebuilt Barkerville after the 1868 fire. The man at lower left confronts historians with a puzzle — Is he barber Wellington D. Moses?

Opposite page: Richfield in 1868. The log building with the flagpole at lower left is the courthouse where Barry was tried, then later hanged on a scaffold in front. The log building was replaced in 1882 by one which is still in use, B.C.'s oldest courthouse.

examine Barry's weapon. But the gambler never let it out of his possession. "Even slept with it under his pillow," Fraser remembered.

Fraser parted company with his dubious companion at Quesnel. It was the same day that Barry made his acquaintance with Moses and Blessing.

After hearing Fraser's story, the picture was clearer in the barber's mind. He decided it was time to go to the police. Next morning in the log-built Richfield police station Moses related his suspicions to Chief Constable W. H. Fitzgerald. The district head of the police listened gravely to the barber's tale.

"A very interesting story, Moses," said Fitzgerald at the conclusion, "and I'll have someone look into it. Meanwhile if you hear anything more. . . ." At that moment he was interrupted by the appearance of Constable John H. Sullivan. "Excuse me, Chief," he said, "but we've just had word from Bloody Edwards' place. They've found a body there. Looks like murder."

"Any identification?" asked Fitzgerald.

"Yes, a man called Blessing. Charles Morgan Blessing. Ever heard of him?"

In the silence that followed Fitzgerald shot a glance at the Barkerville barber. But Moses had turned to gaze out of the window.

The immediate police investigation showed that a miner, out shooting

17

grouse near Edwards' stopping place at Beaver Pass, had been searching just off the road for a wounded bird. Well into the thicket he almost stepped on what he thought was some clothing. But it was clothing that covered what was left of a man. A jacket pocket yielded a wallet, empty of money, but bearing the name of Charles Morgan Blessing. Nearby was a tin cup with the initials "CMB" scratched on the bottom, and at the dead man's feet a clasp knife bearing the same initials. A bullet hole in the back of his skull told the manner of Blessing's end.

As news of the find swept Barkerville, Fitzgerald instructed Sullivan to bring in Barry. But Barry had left — and very suddenly. A warrant was issued, and it was a question of whether to try to catch him at Quesnel or further south at Soda Creek. Sullivan chose the latter and swung into the saddle for a ride of 120 miles (195 km).

When the Constable reined in his sweated mount at the Soda Creek steamboat landing, he learned that Barry had got off the sternwheeler two days before and had promptly taken the six-horse stage to Yale.

Then the quick-witted Sullivan thought of a brand new Cariboo country innovation — the electric telegraph. The Collins Overland Company had only just strung the wire to Quesnel and now for the first time Soda Creek, Yale and New Westminster were in instant communication. The Soda Creek operator tapped out the message that told the B.C. Police at Yale of Barry's flight — the first time the telegraph was used in B.C. to catch a criminal.

Twelve hours later when Barnard's stage pulled into Yale, a police officer was waiting. Barry gave a false name, protesting loudly that the policeman had the wrong man. He ceased protesting when the cell door slammed behind him.

Sullivan was instructed to return Barry to Richfield. During the journey Barry tried to convey to his escort that he'd seen two or three Chinese on the trail after he had parted from Blessing near the Edwards' place. Maybe, he suggested, they had something to do with Blessing's death.

At Barkerville, following the information supplied by Moses, the police traced Blessing's nugget pin to a dance hall girl, who said she had got it from Barry. When the gambler arrived at Richfield, Fitzgerald showed him the pin and asked if it was his.

"Sure it's mine," said Barry.

"Where did you get it?" asked the officer.

"I bought it from a man in Victoria years ago. He went back to the States."

"Ever notice anything peculiar about it?" persisted the officer.

"No," was the nonchalant reply. "It's just a nugget pin."

"That'll be all for the present," said Fitzgerald, a trace of satisfaction in his tone.

In the summer of 1867, Barry was led into the little courtroom at Richfield to face Chief Justice Matthew Baillie Begbie.

As the trial unfolded before a jury of hard-faced Cariboo miners, they heard the dovetailing evidence of Crown witnesses accounting for every movement of Barry at the end of May 1866. Finally to the witness stand came Patrick Gannon, a cattle drover, who said he'd seen Barry and Blessing eating breakfast together by a roadside fire near the Edwards' place just a stone's throw from where the body was found.

The biggest impression was created by the Negro barber, Wellington Delaney Moses, who identified the nugget stick pin handed to him by prosecutor H. P. Walker.

How did he know it was the property of the murdered man?

Because, Moses pointed out, when you looked at it in a certain way you can see the profile of a man's face on one side of the nugget. It was the face on the nugget that he had momentarily seen as he swung the sheet into position under Barry's chin! For proof, the pin was passed for inspection by Judge and jury. They could see the face. In fact, as he held it in his hand, Judge Begbie sketched the pin in his bench book.

Moses had given Fitzgerald this tell-tale clue and Barry, questioned by the police, had fallen into the trap.

The jury said "Guilty." At five o'clock on the morning of August 8, 1866, a gang of men were erecting a scaffold in front of the Richfield courthouse. At seven Barry was hanged, and by eight the scaffold was gone. It was not only a brief execution, it was the first public one in Richfield.

Moses continued his Barkerville business for many years after, and eventually expanded with a sideline of men's and women's wear. Today his barber shop has been restored and is one of several dozen historical exhibits that annually draw tens of thousands of visitors to historic Barkerville.

Moses' Barber Shop in restored Barkerville. "If your HAIR is falling," his sign advises, "call and have it RESTORED before you are baldheaded."
The Barkerville barber died in 1890 and is buried in the Chinese cemetery since the community's main cemetery was reserved for whites.

The Man Who Was Hanged by a Thread

The murdered couple had lain dead in their Peace River cabin for two weeks. Nevertheless, a superb investigation by a B.C. Policeman led to a gallows rendezvous for the killer.

The Peace River district of northeastern B.C. is a big and spacious country, producer of oil and gas and wheat. It is also an area that attracted many people of different nationalities during the pioneer era of the 1920s and 1930s. They were men and women such as the Polish born Babchuks, Joe and Anna, who took up a homestead between Fort St. John and the Beatton River in 1930. Newly married, they had lived in a tent that summer while Joe cut enough poles to build a small one-room log cabin.

The Babchuks settled in their new home in mid-August. Their belongings were few — a cheap iron bed and bedding; a stove, bucket and basin; a rough table and chairs and some shelving. When the couple moved in the gable ends above the wall were open, but Joe figured on finishing them when he had more time, although fate decreed otherwise.

Mike Skakum, a neighbor, noticed the open gables as he walked up to the cabin one afternoon in early September. Mike hadn't seen anything

The Babchuk cabin near Fort St. John where the young couple were murdered. Detective Sergeant W.A. MacBrayne, inset, methodically solved the mystery of the double killing.

of Joe or his wife for a week or two, but thought that since he was going to Fort St. John the next day, the newlyweds might want him to bring something back.

He knocked at the door but there was no answer. He knocked again. Hearing no sound he tried to peer through a window but Anna Babchuk's new scrim curtains blocked the view. Skakum turned his attention to the woodlot where Babchuk cut his firewood. There was no sign of life there.

Puzzled, he wondered if the pair might be ill. He climbed on a water barrel at the end of the house and hauled himself up to look over the open gable into the cabin. When his eyes became accustomed to the gloom, he could see the Babchuks in bed, a dirty canvas tarpaulin covering all but their heads. He yelled at them but they paid no attention. Then he knew why. They were both dead.

Horrified, Mike dropped to the ground, ran to his battered old truck and headed down the gravel road to Fort St. John and Provincial Police Constable Joe Devlin.

"Two dead," thought Devlin, as he scribbled a few notes. "Maybe murder and suicide." Then he called District Sergeant George Greenwood at Pouce Coupe, 50 miles (80 km) away.

In a few hours, the two police officers were tramping across the stubble to the Babchuk cabin. Forcing the door they discovered that the couple had been shot as they lay in bed. The signs indicated that the crime had occurred at least two weeks before. Nearby, on a chair, was an alarm clock, the hands stopped at 4:30.

Propped against a wall was a .30-30 rifle, with one fired shell still in the breech, two live ones in the magazine. From the dirt floor of the gloomy little cabin Sergeant Greenwood retrieved another empty rifle shell. The two policemen noted that Anna Babchuk had lain down on the bed without her shoes but wearing lightweight riding breeches and a sweater. Babchuk was in his underwear; his light grey suit hung over a chair.

Dirty dishes in a tin basin suggested that three people had eaten a meal. Judging the distance of the fired rifle from the bodies, Greenwood deduced that he was dealing with murder, and that the murderer had thrown the tarp over the bodies to ally the suspicion of anyone peering into the cabin.

Greenwood continued a thorough search of the cabin. There was no money in Babchuk's clothing. In fact, there was no money in the cabin. A small wooden trunk attracted the officer's attention but there was nothing much of interest in it except a package of letters written for the most part in Polish.

One, however, was in English from a Mrs. Dron of Beaverlodge, Alberta. It gave Mrs. Babchuk the neighborhood gossip, but there was one remark that Greenwood paid particular attention to: "Wayslki is making some nasty threats and says he's going to kill you both, but you needn't pay any attention to a fellow like him."

It was obvious that something had occurred between the Babchuks and Wayslki in the northern Manitoba town of The Pas, some 300 miles (485 km) northwest of Winnipeg. Mrs. Dron's comment was an interesting lead.

Greenwood notified by radio Divisional Inspector W. V. E. Spiller in

Prince Rupert. Spiller left immediately for Pouce Coupe, although so remote was the Peace River area in the 1930s that he was a week getting there. In the interval Sergeant Greenwood ordered an inquest, preserved the fatal bullets, and generally busied himself trying to pick up the threads of the Babchuk's social life. He could not find any trace of a man called Wayslki in the Peace River.

He did, however, pick up some interesting information from a farmer named Hamilton. He had seen a heavy set, dark man around the Babchuk cabin on several occasions in August. This information led police across the provincial boundary into Alberta to the cabin of Mike Sowry at Hythe.

Sowry told a reasonable story. He'd been very friendly with the Babchuks, he said, and worked for them during August. In fact he helped build the cabin. There were two other men working with him at the time, Sam Burtula and Pete Runka. It appeared that they had all worked at Babchuk's place until August 14 or 15, then left. Sowry was heading for the little community of Hudson's Hope west of Fort St. John when Hamilton saw him. At Hudson's Hope, Sowry made a few purchases, then headed for his home at Hythe. He arrived there August 21. He was sure of the date, and remembered meeting Sam Burtula there and buying him a few drinks in the beer parlor.

While Greenwood and Devlin were in Alberta they took time to interview Anna Babchuk's correspondent, Mrs. Dron at Beaverlodge. She said she had known the Babchuks at The Pas when Annie had been "going steady" with young Wayslki. Then she suddenly dropped him and married Joe Babchuk. Wayslki was furious at being jilted. In fact he was the main reason for the newlyweds leaving Manitoba for the Peace River.

When Inspector Spiller finally arrived at Pouce Coupe and learned of Devlin's enquires, he promptly dispatched a radiogram to headquarters in Victoria suggesting a plainclothes man be sent to check on Wayslki at The Pas. "Tell him to travel by way of Edmonton and I'll meet him there," the Inspector requested.

The man picked was Detective Sergeant W. A. "Bill" MacBrayne, a South African and World War veteran who had followed police work in Western Canada for thirty years. Tall and soldierly, MacBrayne had acquired a unique record in the B.C. Police for solving tough problems. He was briefed on the Peace River killing, then set off for Northern Manitoba.

He soon found Wayslki — a husky young Ukrainian — working as a sectionhand on the Hudson's Bay Railway. He was still bitter about his treatment by the fickle Annie Babchuk, but MacBrayne's close check showed he had not been away from Manitoba for the past twelve months.

While MacBrayne was busy in Manitoba, Sergeant Greenwood had found another of Babchuk's friends — Tom Boichuk, a middle-aged man. He said that on August 16 there had been a get-together at Pete Runka's place, a sort of housewarming for the Babchuks who were present with Boichuk, Mike Sowry and Sam Burtula. During the party Babchuk asked Boichuk to pick up his mail the next time he went into Fort St. John. It was August 22 when Boichuk went in but there was no mail. He called on the Babchuks to tell them but they didn't answer his knock.

Through a chink in the logs he could see a corner of the tarpaulin over the bed and the clock on the chair. "The hands," said Boichuk, "were at 2:15 and the clock must have been going because I checked my watch, and it was the right time."

Boichuk's account narrowed the date of the murder. The police checked Burtula for his version of the housewarming. He confirmed Boichuk's story, and remembered Boichuk offering to bring back the Babchuk mail. And he was sure of the date — August 16.

Did he meet Mike Sowry after that date? Yes, he met Sowry in the beer parlor at Hythe. Mike seemed to have quite a roll of bills and bought a round for everyone. He said he'd just come into town. The date was August 23.

"How are you so sure of the date?" asked Greenwood.

For answer Burtula produced his bank book and pointed to a deposit made that day.

The mystery was deepening. Sowry had claimed the date of his return

Like the Peace River settlers below in 1930, the unfortunate Babchuks hoped to build a life of independence on the land.

to Hythe as August 21. By this time Detective Sergeant MacBrayne had arrived in the Peace River from his Manitoba investigation and quickly noticed a discrepancy in the date of Sowry's homecoming.

The Babchuks were alive on August 16 at Burtula's party, but they could have been dead on August 22 when Boichuk said the alarm clock was running. How long had they been dead? And how long does an alarm clock run?

The police checked back with rancher Hamilton and described Mike Sowry. Yes, that was the man he'd seen around the Babchuks. He last saw him on the afternoon of August 21. The police now realized that Sowry wanted to put himself at Hythe on August 21. He was moving his dates back, but the evidence was against him.

Then Constable Devlin learned that no one around Hudson's Hope had seen Mike Sowry around the middle of August. Furthermore, the storekeeper denied selling him anything.

In the meantime Detective Sergeant MacBrayne had experimented with the Babchuk alarm clock and learned that it ran down in thirty-six hours. If it was running on the afternoon of August 22, then the Babchuks were

The Fort St. John police station where Sowry learned that he had picked up the wrong coat at his victims' cabin.

killed on August 20 or 21. Was this why Sowry wanted to slow down the calendar? Maybe. In any case, it was a purposeful Spiller and MacBrayne who left for Hythe that afternoon to further question Mike Sowry.

Sowry met them at the door with an enquiring look. He was wearing a black work shirt and dark tie which contrasted to his light grey suit. Mac-Brayne thought there was something oddly familiar about that suit. He had seen one like it quite recently, but couldn't remember where.

Sowry's wife listened as the police investigators asked him to repeat his movements in mid August. Sowry related how he had been looking for a homestead and had driven to Pouce Coupe and left his car there. Then he walked by stages to Fort St. John, met the Babchuks and worked as their helper until August 15. He attended Burtula's party on August 16, then went on to Hudson's Hope, sleeping in the bush for two or three nights on the way. After that he headed back home and got to Hythe on August 21.

"Burtula," interposed MacBrayne, "says you were in the Hythe beer parlor on August 23."

"He's mistaken," said Sowry.

"He says you had quite a roll of bills — where did you get the money?"

"I only had a dollar or two," said the uneasy suspect.

MacBrayne suddenly turned to Mrs. Sowry. "When did your husband get back to Hythe?"

"I wasn't here," replied Mrs. Sowry. "I was visiting friends in Beaverlodge."

"Did he give you any money when you got back?" went on MacBrayne.

"Yes, fifty. . . ." she blurted out.

"Fifty what?"

"Fifty dollars." It was almost a whisper.

MacBrayne turned to Sowry. "Where did you get the money, Sowry?"

"I got it from two men," came the halting answer. "Two men I drove from Pouce Coupe to Fort St. John."

"You said you left your car at Pouce Coupe and walked."

There was silence.

Inspector Spiller rose. "Better get your hat, Sowry, you're coming with us."

Before the trio departed in the police car, MacBrayne made a quick check of Sowry's car. The glove compartment yielded a box of .30-30 cartridges. There were four shells missing. And they were the same brand as the empties found at the murder scene.

But still the Detective Sergeant wasn't satisfied. There was the ownership of the rifle. Sowry denied it was his, and Babchuk couldn't talk.

Although the investigation had narrowed the time of the murder to within twenty-four hours, the policemen still hadn't found out who it was who spent the last night with the Babchuks — the mysterious visitor who shared their last meal. And, there was still no clue as to how much money had been in the cabin.

As the police officers drove back to Fort St. John with the murder suspect, something kept disturbing MacBrayne. Something to do with the suit Sowry wore.

Only when they stepped inside the Fort St. John police office did Mac-

Brayne remember why Sowry's suit looked familiar. It was the same sort of grey suit that the murdered Babchuk wore. In fact, it was almost identical. In the police office MacBrayne went casually to the cupboard where the Babchuk exhibits were held. He took out the dead man's coat and pants and studied them closely with a magnifying glass. He took the pants over to the window for a closer look.

Suddenly he turned to Sowry. "Take off your coat, Mike, I want to look at it!"

Bewildered, Sowry did as he was told. MacBrayne studied it in silence — the only sound the ticking of the office clock — then tossed the coat on the table.

"You can lock him up, Joe," he said to Devlin, "and then bring me his pants!"

With Sowry gone, Greenwood and Spiller waited for an explanation.

"Ever hear of a man who went into a restaurant and came out with the wrong hat?"

The two nodded.

"Well," went on MacBrayne, "you've just seen the man who picked up the wrong coat at the scene of a murder."

"You mean . . .? said Greenwood.

"Sure. Sowry is wearing Babchuk's coat. And Sowry's coat is in the exhibit cupboard. They look the same, but Babchuk's suit has a dark thread in it."

At the trial a ballistics expert testified that the gun found in the Babchuk cabin fired the fatal bullets, and that the shells came from the box in Sowry's possession. Sowry had no money prior to August 21, but he displayed a roll of bills in the Hythe beer parlor, and gave his wife $50 when he got home. Apart from his false statements to the police, the most telling piece of evidence was the mix-up in the two grey suits. In his haste to get away after the murder, Sowry, in the dim light of the cabin, had grabbed the wrong coat and left his own in its place.

Reconstructing the crime, the Crown contended that the Babchuks had offered Sowry a meal and a bed on the floor for the night. Mrs. Babchuk, not wanting to undress in front of a stranger, took off her shoes and lay on the bed fully dressed.

When Sowry was sure they were asleep he shot them, took the money and his coat and fled into the night.

When Mike Sowry climbed on to a platform at Oakalla Prison a few minutes before seven on the morning of August 14, 1931, Canada's official executioner might have thought he was adjusting an ordinary rope around the doomed man's neck. But the policemen who had solved the murder knew that the real rope was made of thread — thin dark thread from a murdered man's coat.

Terror at Taylor's Camp

**As the murderer fled pursuing police, he callously killed
and ate his dog. Ironically, he was captured because
his dog wasn't there to warn of the approaching lawmen.**

Jack Myers was tough, no doubt about that. Tough with his tongue, with
his boots and with his fists, and especially tough with a gun in his hand.
Despite his lawless outlook on life, whether sailing into a southeaster, climb-
ing a mountain or knocking a man down, he did it all with equal facility.
Sometimes, but not often, he met his match among the axe-swinging frater-
nity in caulk boots, woollen shirts and "stagged" denims who logged British
Columbia's coastal forests a century ago. They were men who toppled
twenty-storey-high Douglas firs and skidded them in sections to tidewater
with bull teams.

There were five such men with Jack Myers in the log bunkhouse of
Taylor's camp on Read Island at the northern end of the Strait of Georgia
when trouble started that Sunday night of June 25, 1893. It began when
trigger-quick Myers offended "Big Jack" O'Connor, who reacted by yank-
ing a loaded Winchester rifle from the wall. It was the cue for the catlike
Myers to knock the rifle from O'Connor's hands and stick the muzzle of
a .44 Colt in his belly. The impact threw O'Connor into a chair but as he

fell he grabbed the revolver barrel to twist it sidways before it erupted a death dealing slug.

Bob Burns leaped from his bunk to separate the struggling pair, and grasped the revolver across the frame. Three hands strove for the long-barrelled Colt. "Don't shoot, Jack," O'Connor cried as the table and lamp crashed to the floor. Then came the revolver's thunderous report and O'Connor fell back with a groan, a bullet in his chest.

The other bunkhouse inmates, who'd all been drinking, were startled into action by the gunshot. One grabbed the lamp from the floor and re-lit it to look at O'Connor's wound. An hour later he was dead.

The man who fired the gun, Jack Myers, was a man with no conscience. He had been in the United States and boasted of having killed four men. He had also been jailed for stealing logs and later earned another sentence for forgery in Everett, Washington. From here he managed to saw his way to freedom, but Washington became a little too hot when the local sheriff posted a $100 reward for his capture, so Myers crossed the border into B.C.

In June 1893 he landed on Tumbo Island, one of the Canadian Gulf

Opposite page: Jack Myers who caused terror at the coastal logging camp similar to the one in the photo.

A single-action Colt can be fired without pulling the trigger by "fanning" the hammer, even though the cyclinder is immobilized. This crucial evidence convicted Jack Myers.

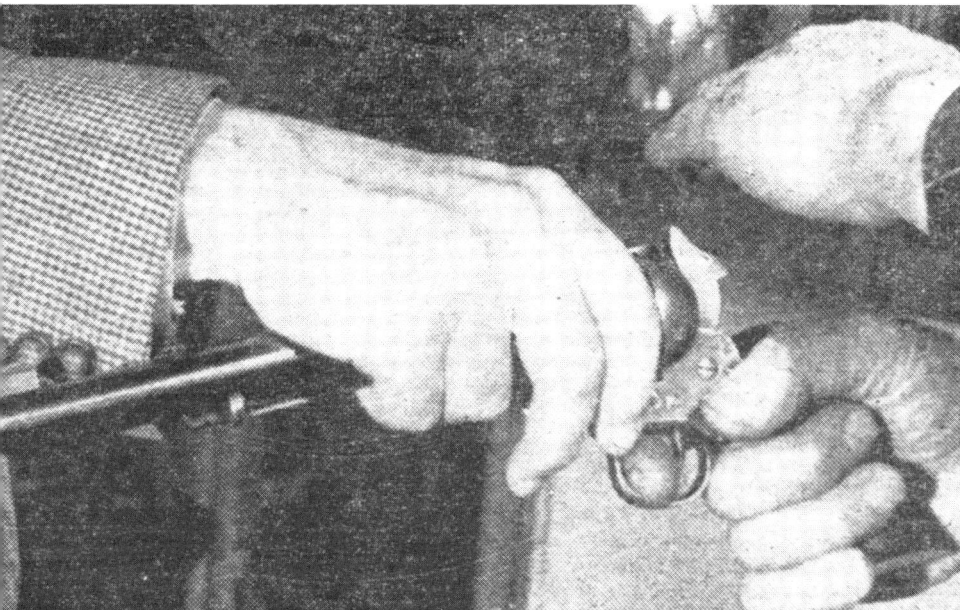

Islands, to complete a deal for a small black and green sailboat. He sailed it across the Strait to Burrard Inlet at Vancouver. After a few discreet waterfront enquires he found on the Inlet's north shore a man with whisky for sale. Myers bought ten cases of "Gaelic" whisky and a case of champagne, and headed up the Strait to begin business as a bootlegger.

His destination was the upper end of the Strait where, in an indescribable tangle of fiords and channels, it could be said "There ain't no Ten Commandments, only men with a thirst." Here the waterways ranged from the broad sweep of a wide channel, slicked here and there with eddies and boilers, down to "hole in the wall" gaps between islands where the muffled roar of the tide-race echoed from sky-scraping cliffs.

In the night before the shooting Myers had dropped anchor in Whitestone Bay at the northwest end of Read Island. Scenting some business, he strolled up the trail to Taylor's camp. In the bunkhouse he found a friend, faller Jack O'Connor.

With a friendly grin, O'Connor extended his hand. "What are you doing away up here, Myers?"

"I don't use that name anymore," was Myers' quiet warning. "Call me Ben. Ben Kennedy." So it was as Ben Kennedy that O'Connor introduced the tough little stranger to the crew — old Salem Hinkley, Angus Cameron, Jack O'Neill and Bob Burns. Myers had the forethought to bring a bottle from his stock and after it had circulated revealed that he had more — at $2 a bottle. The loggers bought, drank, argued and finally slept. Myers returned to his boat.

Next morning someone suggested going out to get a deer. More whisky appeared and eventually O'Connor and Burns set off with Myers in his boat. The expedition produced more drinking than hunting for soon the loggers came staggering back empty handed. Burns, they gleefully reported, fell overboard and had to be retrieved with a boathook.

In the bunkhouse, Hinkley and the others played cards and drank, and by the evening were snoring in their bunks.

Myers had drunk less than the rest, but late that evening he and O'Connor got into a heated discussion about the merits of Myers' terrier dog. "Best bloody watchdog in the country," was Myers' opinion. "Put him to guard something and he never moves."

"I'll bet I'll make him move," was O'Connor's contention, which he backed with a $5 bill. Myers threw his coat on the floor and the dog took up his position. O'Connor's solution was to urinate on the dog which promptly moved. This action so enraged Myers that he drew his .44 Colt and let fly at the dog as it fled for the open door. O'Connor suddenly yanked the Winchester from the wall. "Hey! Hold on there! You can't do that."

Next thing the logger knew the rifle had spun from his hands and he faced the muzzle of Myers' six-gun. Burns interceded. Came the fatal shot and O'Connor died.

Unconcerned, Myers went back to his boat and turned in. The following morning he returned to the bunkhouse to talk things over. He proposed reporting the matter to the Provincial Police, with the story that O'Connor had committed suicide. If the others stuck to the story, he figured all would be well. But the loggers caught the idea that Myers would have a gun in his pocket during the interrogation. The proposal received a sullen reception and Myers realized he wouldn't get any co-operation in his wild scheme. It was probably this attitude of brooding resentment that encouraged Myers to discreetly pick up the Winchester and a shotgun and take them down to his boat. From then on a cat and mouse game went on between Myers and the loggers. Once, for a test, he left his revolver on a bunk while he went over to the stove and made himself some coffee.

"All right, Kennedy, we've got you now!" came a sudden, taunting command. Myers whipped round to size up Burns with the .44 in his fist.

"What are you going to do?" asked Myers quizzically, advancing toward the gun muzzle.

"Going to tie you up and take you in to Comox and hand you over to the police."

"You forgot something," said Myers. "There's no shells in that gun."

Before Burns could check, a lightning punch caught him on the jaw and the gun dropped to the floor.

Monday and Tuesday passed in uneasy stalemate, O'Connor's body in a nearby shed. Finally, on Wednesday morning the men discovered that Burns had left quietly during the night in a skiff. He was on his way to Cortez Island to inform Justice of the Peace Mike Manson of the killing. Burns' action broke the deadlock. Myers hauled up his anchor and sailed out of the bay. The four loggers watched the bootlegger's black-hulled sloop head toward Whitestone Pass.

A few days later, Coroner and Justice of the Peace Manson, with Constable W. B. Anderson of Comox, landed at Read Island to hear the loggers' story, corroborated by the bullet hole in the floor. As he pieced the evidence together, Anderson figured the loggers had consumed sixteen bottles of whisky in twenty-four hours. He noted, too, that Myers had an unusual number of firearms with him — a .38 and a .44 Colt revolver, a .44 Winchester rifle, a shotgun and a .50 caliber Express rifle.

Constable Anderson set out in search of the fugitive and two days later as he approached the shoreline of Ramsay Arm he was challenged by the thunderous report of the Express rifle. He returned the fire and ordered Myers to throw down his gun. His reply was two more shots from the bullgun that caused Anderson to duck for cover. Undeterred, the policeman reconnoitered the rear of Myers' hideout, then he broke in the door of the cabin. It was empty.

Myers had left a couple of empty bottles, "Gaelic" brand, and some firearms and ammunition. But the .44 Colt and the .44 Winchester were gone. The reason was obvious. Myers had taken to the bush with two guns that used the same ammunition.

By now the veteran Anderson had decided that this man-hunt was going to be more than a one-man job. He returned to Comox to telegraph his District Chief at Nanaimo, who reported events to headquarters in Victoria.

As a consequence, the July stillness of Ramsay Arm was disturbed by the whistle of the little coastal freighter *Estelle*. On deck, scanning the shoreline through field glasses, was B.C. Police Superintendent Fred Hussey, accompanied by the Chief Constable from Nanaimo and two Constables.

As part of Hussey's plan, the police were searching for any boats or canoes that Myers might steal to escape.

As they viewed the heavily timbered mountain slope that flanked Ramsay Arm, the police considered Myers was still on the west side of the arm. If he spotted the *Estelle* there was a chance he might attempt to climb the 4,000-ft. (1,200-m) hump of the Downie Range and come down into Bute Inlet. In this case, Myers would have the choice of rafting to Stewart Island, or walking the foreshore to pick up an Indian canoe. Hussey decided to put two men ashore to pick up his trail, while he and the remaining constable, A. F. McKinnon, cruised the Bute Inlet side of the Downie Range. Two thoughts were in Hussey's mind: Myers would have to eat, and he'd have to shoot to eat. In that silent vastness a shot would be heard for miles. Moreover, if he lit a fire, the smoke would be seen.

While these plans were being laid, Myers was heading through the bush, terrier at his heels, the Winchester over his shoulder and the Colt at his hip. It was tough going, angling up hill, under and over deadfalls, through head-high salal and avoiding the vicious spines of luxuriant devil's club. He made a fireless camp the first night high above the shoreline of Ramsay Arm. By the third night he reached the summit. The fourth he spent beneath a tree below the summit on the Bute Inlet side.

By now, Myers was gaunt, trembling with exhaustion and hunger. Rather than risk the noise of a shot, he callously killed his dog with a blow on the head. But if he couldn't risk a shot, he had to risk a fire. Far out in Bute Inlet, Hussey aboard the *Estelle* quickly saw the faint blue wisp of smoke that hovered above the trees. It meant only one thing. Myers was on his way down.

"We'll meet him on the trail," Hussey said to McKinnon. Minutes later the pair jumped into one of the *Estelle's* boats and rowed to shore.

Myers, meanwhile, slung some chunks of half-cooked dog meat over his shoulder and headed downhill. At sunset he lay under a tree for another fireless night, by now only a short distance from shore.

The next morning the two police officers continued their uphill progress, closing the gap between them and Myers. Suddenly Hussey, who was leading, halted and pointed to a stand of hemlock. Standing in the dappled morning light was Myers, rifle in hand, leaning against a tree — and looking the other way. He appeared to be listening, as if some sixth sense told him he was not alone.

There was irony in Myers' situation, for the dog who should have given warning was dead. The animal that had unwittingly provoked murder in his master's heart was now, by its absence, helping to put Myers into police hands.

Less than 100 yards (90 meters) separated Hussey and McKinnon from their quarry. They silently concealed themselves behind a tree as Myers trudged past them down the slope. He'd gone only half a dozen steps when Hussey's "Drop your gun and get your hands up!" startled the killer to an abrupt halt. The Winchester fell to the ground as his hands went skyward and he turned to the men who had outsmarted him.

Myers was soon handcuffed and aboard the *Estelle*. After picking up the two remaining officers the little steamer headed for Comox. There on

July 12, Myers was charged with the murder of Jack O'Connor. Four and a half months later he appeared before Mr. Justice Norman Boles in New Westminster. His defence lawyers were two bright young men, Charles Wilson and Egar A. Magee. Attorney General Theodore Davie, assisted by Deputy Attorney General A. G. Smith, acted for the prosecution.

The jury heard the story of the drunken orgy at lonely Taylor's camp and how Myers propositioned the bunkhouse crew to support the suicide theory. Bob Burns who had gone for help was not present to give evidence. Tragically, he had drowned that August, but his deposition given at the preliminary hearing was admitted as evidence.

The defence's main point was that either O'Connor or Burns in struggling with the gun had caused its accidental discharge. They argued that being a single action Colt, Myers' grip on the trigger could not cock the gun, and an uncocked gun could not be discharged. In any event, claimed the defence, five men drinking sixteen bottles of whisky in twenty-four hours could not be relied upon to describe what did happen, especially when the shooting took place in complete darkness.

To the defence contention about the gun, Theodore Davie said: "There is no one present in this court who will disagree with the fact that the gun was discharged because the hammer fell on the cartridge." He let this reasonable assumption sink in, then added: "And the hammer fell on the cartridge because Myers fanned it with his left hand."

It was an effective way of co-relating the direct evidence that Myers was adept in the handling of firearms, familiar with the western technique of "fanning" the hammer of a single action Colt.

"It was that swift glancing blow with the heel of his left hand," continued Davie, "that cocked and released the hammer in one instantaneous movement and with sufficient leverage to break Burns' grasp on the cylinder." He followed his argument with a convincing demonstration.

The jury was out just over an hour and brought in a verdict of "guilty of manslaughter." Judge Boles sentenced Myers to life imprisonment.

The following year two incidents occurred that reminded the Provincial Police of the drama-packed quest for Jack Myers. In the spring the little steamer *Estelle* blew up off Cape Mudge in a shattering explosion that killed the captain and every member of his crew. Only floating timbers were found to mark the tragedy.

Later in the fall, prisoner Jack Myers in the penitentiary at New Westminster took advantage of a guard's momentary preoccupation to bolt for freedom from a work gang. Disregarding the warning to halt, he was all but through an open gate when a guard's rifle cracked. Myers stumbled and fell. When they picked him up he was dead.

Murder on the Trail of '98

To solve the crime Chief Constable Bullock-Webster became manhunter, coroner, undertaker, preacher, lawyer, and, almost, the hangman.

British Columbia's Provincial Policemen were spread so thin that often one or two were responsible for policing an area larger than many European countries. In addition, they were frequently totally isolated, without a road or even a telegraph line. In the records of the force there are many instances of policemen by their own ingenuity overcoming problems resulting from isolation and a corresponding lack of a doctor, coroner, preacher, jury, undertaker and even a hangman. A good example of these problems — and solutions — is the case of Joseph Camille Claus, a stockily built man who not only had greed in his heart but murder on his mind.

I got the eyewitness account of Claus' downfall over fifty years ago from the late William Howard Bullock-Webster. Though then in law practice in Victoria, he had years before been a member of the B.C. Provincial Police. Bullock-Webster was of a type not uncommon in the early days of the force. Son of an Indian army officer, educated at 400-year-old Sher-

The three men opposite camped at Glenora in May 1898 were typical of some 30,000 who stampeded to Klondike.

Inset: Joseph Camille Claus who murdered his partners.

borne School in England, he came to B.C. in 1886. Six years later he joined the Provincial Police and when the 1897 Klondike rush demanded extra policing in northern B.C., he was posted to the Cassiar country adjoining the Yukon border.

There, as Chief Constable, he had his district headquarters at Glenora, not far from Telegraph Creek on the Stikine River. There were eleven men in his command, holding down detachments at Lake Bennett, Teslin Lake, Echo Cove, Fort Simpson and Port Essington at the mouth of the Skeena River. In all, he was responsible for an area far larger than his home country of England. Worse, the only access to Glenora was by sternwheel steamer during the brief summer months. After that it was by dog team and snowshoes through miles of wilderness.

In the spring of 1898 a six-man party of gold-seekers was checked through Glenora, heading for the Yukon. In the group were Joseph Claus, three Vipond brothers from Nanaimo, B.C., a Norwegian called Jens Hendricksen, and a Scot aptly named Robert Burns.

Hendricksen and Burns, in Western parlance, were "pretty well heeled," with about $1,000 on them. The others, like most of the men stampeding north, had barely enough to live on. All, however, seemed to be travelling in harmony and after a stopover of a day or so moved northward toward the frostbitten Eldorado on the far-off Yukon River. Some time later word came back to Glenora that friction had developed in the party and it had split up, the Viponds deciding to go on alone.

Still later a packer brought word of finding a derelict snow-laden tent about 30 miles (48 km) from Glenora. This news was a circumstance requiring police attention, and Bullock-Webster with Constable Malcolm McLean set off to investigate. Eventually they found the sagging tent and discovered two men who seemed to be asleep. Closer examination, however, showed it was a sleep from which neither would awaken. They proved to be Hendricksen and Burns, the former shot through the head, the latter the victim of ghastly head injuries probably caused by an axe. Their pockets were empty which led Bullock-Webster to consider robbery as the most likely motive.

In his methodical style, the Chief Constable searched for a rifle and possibly an axe. He found neither. Then, along a nearby frozen tributary of the Stikine, he noticed a blow hole in the ice. Underneath was a dark shadow. It was chilly work delving under the ice, but finally Bullock-Webster retrieved a bundle which turned out to be a rifle wrapped in a mackinaw coat.

The killer was smart enough to dispose of the rifle rather than have it found in his possession.

What puzzled Bullock-Webster was the fact that if the party had been reduced to three, where was Claus? Lured elsewhere and murdered like his partners? Were the Viponds responsible and, if so, where were they?

These questions had to be put aside, however, as the police officers tediously sledded the bodies back to Glenora. Then came the task of thawing them out between two roaring fires. Afterwards, Bullock-Webster reluctantly undertook post mortems. Undigested stomach contents revealed that both men had eaten a meal two or three hours before they were killed. It

The Stikine River community of Glenora flared during the 1898 Klondike rush then died when the stampede ended. Above is the remains of the jail in the 1930s.

was probably an evening meal, for the tent was up and they were in their blankets.

In the course of his examination Bullock-Webster probed the bullet from Hendricksen's head. With the aid of a pair of miner's scales and comparison with other unfired bullets, he calculated that the lethal slug came from the rifle hidden under the ice. Though the ballistics test was rough and ready, he could say that the bullet was of matching weight and caliber.

With the medical part of the enquiry finished, Bullock-Webster then became the coroner. Empanelling a jury of miners, he laid the facts before them. The seasoned sourdoughs were unanimous in their verdict: "Murder by a person or persons unknown."

The inquest over, the Chief Constable became undertaker, finishing his busy day by conducting a burial service. Then he reverted to his policeman's role of manhunter.

In due course the Viponds were intercepted and questioned. It was apparent they knew nothing of the murders and possessed nothing belonging to the murdered men. But they did add some information. After the party left Glenora Claus started questioning everything they did. For this reason, in disgust the Viponds went their own way.

This scrap of information intrigued Bullock-Webster. Maybe Claus wanted the Viponds out of the way. He could handle two men in a stealthy attack but not five. Bullock-Webster immediately sent word over the Yukon Telegraph Line to pick him up. Some time later Claus mushed in to Teslin Lake — right into the arms of Provincial Constable Arthur D. Drummond. Claus, who had been penniless at Glenora, was now found to have about

$1,000 on him . . . in a purse that belonged to one of the dead men! Asked about the money he had an ingenious explanation. Seems that one night Burns flew into a violent rage and shot Hendricksen, then turned his rifle on Claus — who was just nimble enough to snatch up an axe and defend himself. Burns got the worst of it.

After that, said Claus, he took their money for safe-keeping and was going to hand it over to the first policeman he met.

When Claus was escorted back to Glenora a few legal problems developed which threatened to prevent a trial. The Attorney-General's Department had arranged for Mr. Justice Walkem to go to Glenora, accompanied by Crown counsel and a lawyer for the defence. By a quirk in the immigration treaty between Britain and the United States, however, the legal party could not trans-ship through Alaskan territory to British Columbia.

Meantime, Bullock-Webster had collected miners to act as jurymen. They were not happy since they wanted to be on their claims for the spring breakup. With the trial apparantly delayed, they decided to leave. Bullock-Webster, however, quickly displayed the ingenuity — and a little law bending — often necessary in far-flung police outposts. He "conjured" up a batch of subpoenas, attached large red seals, then slapped a paper in the hands of each prospective juryman. Blandly he warned them that if they left the settlement they would face a six-month jail term!

Bullock-Webster had even prepared for the possible final eventuality — Claus' conviction and hanging. Years later he told me he had bought a rope from the Hudson's Bay Company and arranged for the use of their fur loft for the execution.

"Who on earth was going to hang him?" was my interested query.

"Oh," said Bullock-Webster in his quiet fashion, "I figured I would have to do it. After all, I performed all other functions."

He was spared the possible duty of hangman when word arrived that there would be no Assize in Glenora. In addition to the immigration problem, there were an insufficient number of registered voters in the Cassiar and no jury could be empanelled. Claus would be tried in Nanaimo. The miners "subpoenaed" by Bullock-Webster happily scattered to their claims.

In late June 1898, a jury of Nanaimo businessmen and coal miners listened with rapt attention to a story of murder and robbery in the frozen wasteland that bordered the mighty Stikine River. Claus was found guilty and sentenced to hang on August 14.

On the eve of his execution a guard noticed Claus acting strangely in his cell, but by the time help arrived the prisoner was in a coma. Apparently he had taken some deadly poison, although where he got it remained a mystery. Some thought he had brought it with him from the north, secreted in the lining of his coat or the cuff of his pants. Others felt it might have been between the pages of a Bible his wife gave him the day before.

Whatever the answer, it was the last act in one of the many tragedies that marked the Trail of '98. There was, however, something of a sequel. While Chief Constable Bullock-Webster had been spared the duty of hanging his prisoner, as related in the next chapter, Constable J.L. Crimp was not so fortunate.

Oration from the Gallows

**As Constable Crimp adjusted the noose around Johnson's
neck the murderer was more concerned with
giving advice to the spectators than with dying.**

Some rotting timbers half hidden among the undergrowth where Dease
Creek runs into Dease Lake are all that remain of Laketon in the Cassiar
region of northwestern B.C. Spawned by the Cassiar gold rush over a century ago, it was once the "Metropolis of the Cassiar" — at least by the
standards of the sparsely populated north. In summer its population soared
to as many as 300, but in winter dwindled considerably as everyone who
could left its harsh climate for the south. Laketon's winter population was
described in one report as: "Two hotelkeepers, three butchers, four whip-

The remains of the courthouse at the abandoned community of
Laketon in the 1930s. The inset photo is of Judge Crease who in
1877 conducted the Assizes from a stretcher after his horse had
fallen on him.

sawyers, 18 miners, a teamster and 'our enlightened and well-informed policeman and seven petty larceny poker players wasting their time at four-bit limit'.''

Laketon was also the scene of the last Assize ever held in the Cassiar and where a Provincial Policeman had to substitute for the hangman. The culprit, an Indian named Ciah-a-Kah, but more popularly known as Johnson, made what was probably the longest farewell speech at a B.C. hanging — and the most moving. Furthermore, his words were recorded by an old bottle-scarred newspaperman apparently called John who had worked on the *New York Herald* before the U.S. Civil War of the early 1860s.

At the time of the hanging in 1879 six years had passed since a man from Minnesota named Thibert crossed the Rockies to find himself in unexplored country some 70 miles (113 km) northeast of Telegraph Creek on the Stikine River. Here in 1873 he discovered gold on the creek that bears his name, sparking a rush that netted $2 million in two brief seasons and giving rise to settlements like Glenora and Telegraph Creek on the Stikine, and Laketon, McDame Creek and Centreville.

With the miners came the law and by the time Johnson had got himself enmeshed in the statutes, Provincial Constable J. L. Crimp was stationed at Laketon, Bob Pool at McDame Creek, and James Normansell at Glenora. It was typical — three policemen to patrol a maze of mountains without a mile of road, where snow could fall anytime and dog teams and horses were the main means of travel — for the fortunate. Most miners had neither dog team nor packhorse and relied on snowshoes in winter, boots in summer.

It was a land that played no favorites. In 1877, for instance, Judge H. P. P. Crease's horse fell on him as he rode to Laketon to hold the Assize. The Judge was carried the rest of the way strapped to a stretcher, and from a stretcher in the Laketon courtroom he conducted the Assize.

Another stretcher case that winter was Hawaiian freighter Bill Kanahana who failed to show up at Dease Lake one week in January. He was found on the trail unconscious and covered with snow, hands and feet badly frozen. In temperatures that dropped to -40°F (-40°C) and colder, volunteer searcher Dick Glenn pulled the stricken man 90 miles (145 km) in four days to Laketon's hotelkeeper Joe Clearihue who nursed Bill slowly back to health.

Some of the characters who had known other gold strikes such as Wild Horse in the East Kootenay appeared on the Cassiar scene. They were men like "Dancing Bill" Latham — who opened a dance hall with four Indian women and a hand organ.

The only white woman in Laketon was Nellie Cashman, a young petite Irish blonde who hauled her sleigh-load of supplies up the Stikine in February to make Dease Lake in twenty-seven days. There she built a hotel and ran it for two seasons. When last heard of in 1898, she was outfitting in Victoria for the Klondike.

This was the pattern of Cassiar society when one evening in the summer of 1879, Johnson went looking for his wife among the riverside shacks and cabins that made up Telegraph Creek on the Stikine River. Johnson was an American Indian from Fort Wrangel, Alaska, where, apparently, he'd picked up some loose ideas about gun-toting and law enforcement, and his wife, Susie, some wayward habits.

This evening as Johnson tried to find her, it seemed that everywhere he enquired she was somewhere else.

"I saw her with a white man behind Brierly's Saloon," cracked one wag to the morose brave. By the time Johnson's moccasined feet had taken him through the alley behind Brierly's, someone else reported Susie in another direction.

"Saw her down on the steamboat," said someone, "running away with another Indian. Better hurry if you want to catch her."

Off went Johnson to the sternwheeler about to cast off for Wrangel. Susie wasn't aboard, and a freight-handler cut short his search by kicking him off the boat.

Perhaps it was this last indignity that fanned Johnson's rage. By the time he found Susie he was ready for murder.

"You come with me!" he growled, as he dragged her by the arm down the dusty main street. Finally, Susie sat down and would go no farther.

"You go 'way, leave me alone," she muttered. And she was just in time to duck the flashing blade of Johnson's knife that would have scalped her.

Ken Morris, a miner, saw the incident and rushed over to grab Johnson.

In the lurching struggle between the two, the Indian managed to pull a revolver and fire a shot. It didn't hit Morris, but the explosion burned his coat.

About this time George Jenkinson — toll collector at Telegraph Creek — crossed the street to give Morris a hand. Jenkinson recoiled with a groan as Johnson's knife caught him below his ribs. As he staggered back, clutching his side, Morris managed to trip the Indian. As they rolled on the ground he wrenched the revolver from Johnson's grip.

Regaining his feet, he threw the gun in a nearby creek. As the Indian advanced on him, Morris caught him off guard and threw him in the creek.

It was now that Morris felt a pain in his thigh and, figuring he'd been shot, made for Harris' Saloon. At the entrance he fell flat on his face. The wound proved to be a stab from Johnson's knife.

Meantime, out in the street, Jenkinson had sunk to the ground. In a matter of minutes he was dead.

Three miners passing by decided to carry Jenkinson to his cabin, but as they lifted him, Johnson reappeared, knife in one hand, revolver in the other. At the sight of Johnson's slow, menacing approach, the good Samaritans dropped Jenkinson's body and retreated.

Susie now appeared, trying to stay the mad course of her husband's anger, but it was no use. Johnson threw her off and fell to stabbing the prone figure of Jenkinson.

Susie averted her head at the sight, she said in evidence later, but heard the thudding blows.

"I'm going to kill another white man!" yelled Johnson, as he scrambled to his feet. And Susie again tried to hold him back. A group of whites who had collected attracted Johnson's attention. He would have fired into them had not Susie told him there were Indian children nearby.

The sternwheeler *Strathcona*, shown at Telegraph Creek in 1898, was typical of the one from which Johnson was booted off in 1879 as he searched for his wayward wife.

One of the bystanders made a move toward Callbreath's house, the only man in the settlement with a revolver. But he didn't have any shells. He did, however, have a breech-loading Remington rifle, but by the time a small posse was formed, Johnson had disappeared. Their quarry gone, the group decided to send for the police. Someone set off down the Stikine River 9 miles (14 km) to Glenora. Back came Constable Normansell with two Special Constables, Barney Johnson and Fred Lynch.

The trio quickly picked up Johnson's trail and after a day's hard travelling caught up with him high above the Stikine River. After an exchange of shots, Johnson raced downhill to a dry stream bed. Two officers followed but Normansell, hoping to get ahead of the fugitive, kept to the trail. His strategy paid off and the policeman found himself barring Johnson's path. He dashed for the cover of some willows.

"Come out or I'll shoot!" was the Constable's crisp order.

Johnson slowly appeared. Normansell could see that in the exchange of shots earlier in the day, the Indian had caught a slug in the shoulder. His left arm hung useless at his side.

"I want to tell you about my troubles," Johnson said.

"You can tell them to me in jail," was the lawman's rejoinder.

"All right, I go to jail." Johnson shambled towards the muzzle of Normansell's gun. Then his knife flashed. The sweeping blade sliced Normansell's coat and shirt before the officer could grab the Indian's wrist and swing him on his back. Even with his disabled arm and shoulder, Johnson again and again tried to attack Normansell. There was only one

42

thing to do, and Normansell did it. He belted Johnson with his gun butt until the man lost consciousness.

The trial of Johnson opened before Justice Matthew Baillie Begbie in the Glenora courtroom on August 29, 1879. As Johnson was undefended, Judge Begbie ordered a plea of "not guilty." Theodore Davie represented the Crown, and one by one the witnesses told their story. The verdict was "guilty," with Johnson sentenced to hang.

The scaffold that Provincial Constable Crimp built in the little jail yard at Laketon late that September had its platform higher than the surrounding fence. For this reason Indians who gathered from near and far and the few local whites had a good view of the sentenced man when he climbed the steps at 8 o'clock on the crisp and frosty morning of October 1.

Crimp, filling in as executioner, adjusted the rope. There was a delay because Johnson wished to speak.

"My dear friends," he said, "there are many white men who do wrong to the Indians, and many Indians who do wrong to whites. I should like all this ill-feeling to stop and I want you all to help to bring it about. Take pity on the poor Indians! Look at me, think of what will happen to me today. See what I have come to! Have no trouble and do no wrong to white men. Do not be downhearted at what will befall me today but turn your hearts to God."

From the crowd, an Indian woman screamed in the Casca tongue: "Don't talk too much; die at once. I am not afraid to see you die. My heart is strong. Make yours strong, too, and die quickly."

In resignation, Johnson called: "Kitty, stop talking. Don't be afraid for me. Strengthen your heart."

Then he looked back at those around him and went on:

"Friends, tell all my friends at Fort Wrangel to pray for me. Tell them I said this without fear or trembling; I am not afraid to die. I have prayed to God to forgive me. While I stand here I think of all the great white chiefs I have been told of, Queen Victoria, Washington and others. They are all good people."

He turned for a moment to glance over the fence, with an enquiring, "Are you there, John?"

An answering voice said, "Yes."

"John, it is good for you to let everyone, white and Indian, know what I have said. I will not shame my people; I will not ask for mercy. John, I do not want to be buried here. My dying wish is to be buried in my own country, among my own people."

At that moment Crimp made a move to pinion the condemned man's wrists. Johnson said something like, "Bye and bye," and asked for the rope to be slackened. He knelt and made the sign of the Cross. Then, slowly regaining his feet, said, "Go ahead."

They were his last words.

The *Beryl G.* on which father and son were murdered; and hi-jackers Owen Baker, top, and Harry Sowash.

Hi-Jack Route to the Hangman

During prohibition in the United States smuggling liquor from Canada where its sale was legal yielded racketeers hundreds of millions of dollars. Many, however, didn't die of old age.

During the 1920-33 Prohibition Era in the United States liquor smuggling from Canada, where the sale of liquor was legal, grew into an incredibly profitable venture. Involved were not only individuals but also gangs controlled by criminals such as the notorious killer Al Capone, whose illegal activities in 1927 alone earned him an estimated $107 million. Stemming from this booze bonanza were thousands of murders since gang warfare was common and hired killers cheap. But these killings weren't restricted to gangs. Lesser hoods could be equally ruthless, as demonstrated by Baker and Sowash in the waters off southern Vancouver Island.

Owen W. Baker was tall and gangly, with an Adam's apple that moved convulsively in his scrawny throat. A lock of hair falling over his forehead gave him a folksy look that belied the savagery he later revealed.

Harry "Si" Sowash, somewhat younger, with his crew cut, broad shoulders and rugged build could have been taken for a university football player. In keeping with this academic impression, he read a lot and knew his way around in Greek and Roman history. He also had a sense of humor. After dictating and signing a lengthy murder confession, he passed it to Provincial Police Inspector Tom Parsons with the remark: "A good caption for that would be 'The Toilers of the Sea'."

I remember, as the pair awaited their execution, that Baker wrote to all his relatives and acquaintances pleading for money and legal assistance for a last-minute appeal. Sowash, on the other hand, wrote only one letter — to the manufacturers of a well-known brand of shaving cream. They had originated a new sales gimmick which consisted of a little chain to prevent the cap from going astray.

Sowash wrote the company telling them how, for years, he had been troubled by the cap falling into the drain hole of the wash basin. In satirical vein he thanked them for this boon to shavers. Of course, the company could not have known that their correspondent had just two weeks to live.

Baker met Sowash while he was doing a five-year stretch for white slavery in McNeill Island Penitentiary in Washington. Sowash was serving two years for selling stolen airplane parts.

When the pair were released it was the heyday of rum running and Baker promptly got involved. Equipping himself with a yachtsman's peaked cap, a blue blazer with double row of brass buttons, flashlight and a phony police badge, he intercepted the "rummies" as they unloaded a speedboat in the dead of night along some lonely Puget Sound beach.

His shout, "United States Customs! Stay where you are!" was the cue for the rum runners to flee, leaving their booze which Baker "confiscated."

But he was also adaptable, quickly changing his method of operation to suit circumstances. For instance when a man with four cases of Scotch in the back of his car stopped for a traffic light in mid-town Tacoma, Baker drove up and flashed his badge. After he had handcuffed the unfortunate man to his steering wheel, he fled with the Scotch.

Baker soon learned, however, that the booze business could be hazardous. Once he sold a Seattle man ten cases of gin that proved to be water. Unfortunately for Baker, the purchaser, accompanied by a couple of grim-faced pals, accidentally ran into him on a Seattle street corner. Confronted with his duplicity, Baker simulated amazement.

"You don't say!" he gasped. "Well, it just happens the guy who sold me that gin is around the corner. I'll go and get him."

Baker quickly retreated to the sanctuary of the Commodore Hotel where, in the basement, he burrowed his way into a sawdust pile used for the heating plant. From this hideout his aroused customers dragged him half an hour later, and escorted him upstairs to a fourth storey room. Here they held him by the ankles over the window ledge until he gave assurance of immediate reimbursement. All of which gives some idea of the hazards of the bottle trade in the roaring twenties.

After this alarming episode, but obviously still intent on staying in the liquor business — however hazardous — Baker chartered a fish boat. Picking as accomplices Sowash and a new man, Charlie Morris, he cruised the shoreline of southern Vancouver Island looking for liquor caches which he hoped to steal. The trouble was that after a week of cruising they came up with not a drop.

Then off Sooke Harbour the trio spotted a big, slow-moving fish packer heading in the direction of Victoria. Baker's interest was aroused. It wasn't long before he learned that she was the *Beryl G* out of Vancouver, B.C. But instead of fish she was on a booze shuttle run carrying 600 cases a trip from the *Comet*, an old rusty British freighter anchored beyond the three-mile limit off Vancouver Island's west coast. The skipper and owner of the packer was Bill Gillis of Vancouver who had on board his teenage son, Bill.

The *Beryl G* usually anchored in a cove on the east side of Sidney Island, not far from Victoria, where she disposed of her load to speedy American craft owned by Pete Marinoff of Tacoma. When her hold was empty, the *Beryl G* chugged back to the *Comet* for another load, at the going rate of $6 a case.

About a week later in a room in the New England Hotel on Victoria's Government Street, Baker outlined the intricacies of the old customs racket to Sowash and Morris. Once they were aboard the *Beryl G*, a peaked cap and brass buttons would overawe Gillis and son to mere onlookers as their cargo was removed.

The plan included hiring a Victoria fisherman and his boat, and the next night the trio embarked from the Cadboro Bay Yacht Club and headed for Sidney Island. Here Baker and Sowash rowed over and boarded the *Beryl G*. but the plan went awry, for Gillis appeared with a rifle. Baker promptly shot and killed him.

The unexpected sound of gunfire from the *Beryl G* made the fisherman and Charlie Morris uneasy. Then out of the gloom came Baker, furiously rowing the skiff. He gave sharp instruction to the pair to bring the fishboat alongside and lash it to the *Beryl G*.

As the fishboat got close, they saw young Gillis being herded along the deck by Sowash, who suddenly struck down the youth from behind. "The cold-blooded murderers!" muttered Morris to the fisherman.

With Baker and Sowash in command, there was no time for argument. The *Beryl G's* anchor was hauled up and as the fishboat towed the packer out of the bay, the two men discussed what they should do with the bodies. Baker's answer was to handcuff them together, lash them to the *Beryl G's* anchor and throw them overboard. That is what happened.

Since they had far too much liquor to handle at one time, they cached it here and there along the shoreline, some of it below low water mark, to be retrieved at a later date.

Finally, the bloody night's work done, the fisherman was forced to take Baker, Sowash and Morris to Anacortes in Washington. Then he returned to Victoria, stunned at the turn of events he had unwittingly been pressed into. He decided, unfortunately, to keep silent. The bloodstained and abandoned *Beryl G* was found idly drifting with the tide in Haro Strait.

She was towed to Victoria where B.C. Provincial Policemen boarded her. They began their investigation by analyzing the blood stains on the deck, finding the owner's identity, his business and habits. In the pilothouse a camera yielded a role of film which, after being developed, showed one of Marinoff's boats leaving the *Beryl G*. Marinoff, in turn, was able to pinpoint the moment when one of his boats lifted the last load from the ill-fated craft.

In the weeks that followed, police combed the Victoria and Seattle waterfronts, and learned that Baker and Sowash had hired a Seattle craft to look for liquor cached in the Canadian islands. The liquor had been sold, but through dogged police work the individual purchasers were found. The brands tallied with Gillis' cargo.

Then the unfortunate Victoria fisherman was found, and he finally told the whole story. Warrants were issued. The first man captured was Charlie Morris in Seattle.

It took many months to locate the other two. Finally Baker was found working on a dredge in New York harbor, and Sowash was rounded up in New Orleans. Both paid for their night's work on the gallows, while Charlie Morris got a life sentence.

From then on because of the efficiency of the B.C. Provincial Police and the gallows end of Baker and Sowash, hijackers avoided Canadian waters. Finally, the 1933 repeal of prohibition in the U.S. ended the lucrative trade of booze running. Al Capone, by the way, did not escape either. Although he had killed many men himself, nothing could be proved and he was jailed on an income tax evasion charge. But fate dealt him a harsher sentence. He died a lingering death from syphilis.

Vince Macchione.

The Clue of the Kids and the Candy

Some beer bottle caps, shotgun shell wads and candy bar wrappers weren't much of a clue. Nevertheless, Corporal D.A. McDonald and District Sergeant Andy Fairbairn wove them into a hangman's knot.

Murder victim
Mike Hudock.

Steve Drevenuk, a Fernie miner, discovered the body on Monday morning, February 10, 1936, about 4 miles (6.5 km) from Fernie. It lay below the highway at a point where the Elk River swings toward the road. The temperature was below zero, the early morning sun cast long blue shadows on the frozen, snow-covered landscape. Drevenuk at first thought the figure lying face down near the river bank was a drunk. Then he decided to check, realizing that anyone, drunk or sober, who slept beside a river in sub-zero weather would soon be a corpse.

At that moment he heard a car coming and flagged it down. Together he and the driver scrambled down the bank to discover that the body was already a corpse — and frozen stiff.

Minutes later they were telling their story to Corporal D. A. McDonald of the Fernie detachment of the B.C. Provincial Police. McDonald at 47

The courthouse at Vernon where
the final trial was held.

was a husky, twenty-four-year veteran on the force. After making arrangements with the undertaker and coroner, he accompanied Drevenuk to the scene. McDonald studied the area carefully. Before going down the bank he stooped and picked up two pieces of paper — the crumpled remains of candy bar wrappers. Something else he noticed were two beer bottle caps. These he also pocketed.

Then a few steps down the bank he picked up a cardboard disc about the size of a quarter. The printing on it showed it was a wad from a 16-gauge shotgun shell. At the river's edge, as he knelt beside the dead man, the coroner and undertaker arrived. The three men turned the body over.

The dead man appeared to be about 35 with dark hair. There were spots of blood on his chin and a ragged hole where a shotgun charge had torn into his throat. Near him was a cheap brown cloth cap, six empty beer bottles, some beer caps and another shotgun wad. They could gain nothing from the footprints because local fishermen had trampled the snow. A search of the dead man's clothing revealed two government letters addressed to Mike Hudock of Michel, a small coal mining town 25 miles (40 km) from Fernie. The letters indicated Hudock had been a welfare recipient.

"Hudock?" thought McDonald as he picked up his office phone to report to District Sergeant Andy Fairbairn at Cranbrook. "That name sounds familiar."

Then he remembered that the previous afternoon a Canadian Pacific Railway policeman had phoned to say he had two lost children on his hands. McDonald had driven over to the station to pick them up. The oldest, 9, said his name was Sammy Hudock and he lived at Michel. The puzzled McDonald asked Sammy how he and his brother got to the CPR station.

"Vince took us there," was the cheery response.

"Vince who?"

"Vince Macchione. He knows my dad and mum. He took us to the station in his car and said he'd pick us up later, but he didn't come back."

At the sound of the name, McDonald recalled that he had had previous contact with Vince Macchione — a section hand, he thought, who lived at Galloway some 22 miles (35 km) to the west.

Leaving the children in the police station, McDonald walked up town in search of him. It was about 5:15 when he caught sight of Macchione driving a blue coupe. But before the police officer could flag him down, Macchione had turned left down a side street. McDonald followed until, opposite the Royal Hotel, he noticed Macchione pull to the curb on the other side of the street.

As the police officer crossed the street, he also noticed a woman emerge from a doorway and get into the coupe. McDonald had a talk with her. She was the mother of the lost children and glad to hear they were safe. Macchione seemed glad, too. Apparently an old friend of the Hudocks, he had been delayed and got back to the railway station to find the kids gone. With smiles all round, he drove Mrs. Hudock and McDonald to the police station to pick up the children. After this explanation Corporal McDonald considered the incident closed. But it was to remain closed only until the next day.

A few hours after the discovery of Hudock's shot-riddled body,

Sergeant Fairbairn arrived at the Fernie police office and listened to McDonald's story of death on the bank of the Elk River and the coincidence of meeting Mrs. Hudock and Macchione the day before. Here McDonald paused. Had Hudock been lying dead off the highway while he was speaking to Mrs. Hudock about her children yesterday afternoon?

McDonald had already phoned the Police Constable at Natal and asked him to break the news to Mrs. Hudock. After that he phoned the Constable at Wardner, telling him to go over to Galloway and see what Macchione had to say.

Just after lunch Macchione appeared at the Fernie office with Robert Evans, Mrs. Hudock's brother. "I'm sure sorry to hear about Mike," Macchione told McDonald. "He was one of my best friends. I was only with him yesterday afternoon."

As the conversation developed it seemed that Macchione had been seeing a lot of the Hudocks. The family, he said, had been having a rough time with Mike being on welfare. He'd given them a little money now and again. Last Saturday night he had bought them a week's supply of groceries, then taken the family to Fernie's Northern Hotel for dinner. On Sunday Macchione drove the family into Fernie again, and Mike had left them to meet someone. That was the last they saw of him.

"I figured," Macchione concluded, "he got tied up with some fellows in a hotel room, and would come home later."

That evening at the inquest, a coroner's jury rendered the verdict that Hudock had been killed by a charge of shot that entered his throat. It had been fired at close range and wasn't self inflicted. It was murder.

McDonald's first problem was to find the person who last saw Hudock alive. Persistent enquiries, however, produced nothing. Sergeant Fairbairn was inclined to the "woman" angle and went to Michel to interview Annie Hudock.

Her story was simple. She and her husband and two children had driven to Fernie on Sunday in Vince's car to buy bottled beer. First they tried the Waldorf but the hotel hadn't any. Then they parked outside the Royal and she and her husband went inside while Vince and the kids stayed in the car. The woman at the Royal said she had no bottled beer, but they could have beer by the glass.

"Go and tell Vince to leave the kids in the car and come on in," Mrs. Hudock had told her husband. Hudock went to the car, spoke to Macchione and then, instead of returning to the hotel, walked slowly down the street. Vince followed with the car.

"I thought it funny," said Mrs. Hudock, "because Vince had given us the money to buy the beer. I never saw Mike after that," she concluded, sadly.

"What did you do then?" continued Fairbairn.

"Well," said Mrs. Hudock, "in maybe half an hour when they didn't come back, I went out to look for them."

She said she found Macchione parking his car across the street from the Royal Hotel. Just as she was asking where Mike and the kids had got to, Constable McDonald had walked over and told them the children were at the police station.

"Did Vince say where Mike went?" queried Fairbairn.

"Well, he said he was going to see some man and just walked off."

"And how did the children land at the CPR station?"

"Vince said the kids wanted to run around, so he dumped them off at the station and said he would pick them up later. Then he went looking for Mike and I guess he was late in coming back."

In a way it was a dove-tailing story, although Fairbairn couldn't help wondering why Hudock hadn't returned to the hotel to drink his beer. What made him change his mind and walk down the street? And how, in a small town like Fernie, did Vince Macchione lose track of him? It was curious, too, that Annie Hudock didn't seem to be unduly burdened with grief. But perhaps she was the type that allowed little room for display of grief or affection.

Meantime, McDonald, intrigued by the Hudock-Macchione relationship, decided to have a talk with the dark-eyed Italian.

"You thought a lot of the Hudocks?" was his opening statement.

"I sure did — my best friends."

McDonald thought quickly. Suppose Macchione was attracted to Annie Hudock? Standing treat and buying groceries would be one way of capturing her affections. He'd try it.

"I guess you didn't like to see Mrs. Hudock so poor. Is that why you bought the groceries?"

"I guess that's about it," admitted Macchione.

"Maybe," ventured McDonald, "you liked Annie a little better than Mike?"

"Yes, I guess I did."

"So, I guess you saw a lot of her," continued the Corporal, "maybe sometimes when Mike wasn't around?"

"Sometimes," came the halting admission.

It wasn't much of a clue, but it might lead to a motive. Within an hour McDonald was at Mrs. Hudock's with more questions. One was a leading one. Had Vince Macchione ever shown her any marked affection?

Yes, McDonald learned. In fact Vince had wanted to marry her, and once urged her to leave Mike and go with him to the States. Sometimes he gave her money for dresses. Macchione and Annie Hudock had been more than good friends for a couple of years.

After comparing notes with McDonald, Fairbairn decided to act. Late that night Vince Macchione was arrested at his Galloway home on a charge of murder. He was in bed when McDonald arrived and by the light of an oil lamp sat up as the policeman searched the room for a shotgun.

"You've got a gun here, where is it?" snapped McDonald.

"I haven't got a gun . . . I never owned one," vowed Macchione.

"This yours?" asked McDonald, going through the pockets of an overcoat hanging over a chair.

"Sure it is," said the little Italian.

"Did you wear it last Sunday?"

"Sure."

"Then why were you carrying these?" asked McDonald as he produced two 16-gauge shells.

As part of his plot, Vince Macchione arranged for the unsuspecting Mrs. Hudock to be drinking beer at the Hotel Royal while he murdered her husband.

"I never saw them before," said Macchione, but in a low, unconvincing tone.

On a shelf above the stove were two boxes of 16-gauge shells.

"Why did you get these shells if you haven't got a gun?" probed McDonald relentlessly, as Macchione dressed.

"I don't know how they got there," was the answer.

McDonald took him out to the lean-to garage and spent the next few minutes looking over a blue coupe. Under the front seat were two more 16-gauge shells.

"I guess you don't know anything about these?" remarked the cynical policeman.

"Never saw them before," was the routine answer.

Even with Macchione under lock and key, there were still gaps in the case. Absence of the murder weapon prompted Fairbairn to put gangs of men exploring the culverts along the highway, probing snow drifts, and searching the river bank. Nothing was found. Men who had worked with Macchione on the section gang were interrogated.

"Sure Vince owned a shotgun," said Fred Kalt. "He bought it mail order from Eaton's. He picked it out of the catalogue."

"I saw him with it lots of times," said Bill Lagoda. "It was about 16-gauge."

"I delivered it to him," added Leon Simmons.

A body, a motive, a weapon, and a question: Could Macchione take his victim 4 miles (6.4 km) out of town, shoot him, and return so quickly? On a practice run the officers found they could reach the scene, driving

53

25 to 30 miles (40 to 48 km) an hour, in seven minutes. A fast driver could do it in three or four. One piece of the puzzle was in place. Another was the shotgun wads at the scene. Then there were the beer bottles. They might yield a clue. They were labeled Fernie Brewing Company, but where did Macchione get them? And on a Sunday?

McDonald canvassed the licensed hotels and beer parlours but met with negative replies until he asked Joe Perri of the Central.

"Sure. Vince was in here Saturday," said Perri. "He paid a small bill and asked me to set aside six bottles of beer in a paper bag. Said he would pick 'em up Sunday."

"And did he?"

"Yep. Came in Sunday afternoon just after four o'clock and picked them up. Mike Hudock was with him."

Interesting, thought McDonald. Macchione knew that no bottled beer was going out of licensed premises in Fernie on a Sunday, so he made sure on Saturday that there would be bottled beer for Sunday. It was solid evidence.

Now McDonald had to prove that the blue coupe and its two occupants were on the highway on Sunday afternoon. Could it be done? Word was spread that the police wanted to see anyone who had noticed a blue coupe on the Fernie highway on Sunday, February 9. Incredibly, the next day four men appeared at the Fernie police station. They were electrical workers who had driven to Fernie that Sunday from Elko. Four miles (6.4 km) from Fernie they had seen a blue coupe parked on the right hand side of the road near the river. There was nobody in the car, so they concluded the driver was fishing. They had not noticed the license number.

Fairbairn, still working on his "woman" theory, checked with Annie Hudock to see if they had called on anyone on the way back to Michel that fatal Sunday night. He learned they had dropped in to see the Sowchuks at Hosmer. Mrs. Sowchuk remembered the visitors: Annie Hudock, Macchione and the two kids. They said they'd been to Fernie, then unexpectedly Mrs. Hudock started to cry. Julia Sowchuk followed her into the bedroom and, putting her arm around her, asked what the trouble was.

"Mike's dead," Annie Hudock moaned, between sobs.

"You're crazy!" had been Mrs. Sowchuk's retort. "Mike probably went off with a bunch of fellows and got drunk."

Fairbairn's hunch about the "woman" angle suddenly became overpowering. He quickly returned to Annie Hudock's. What had she meant by that remark at Hosmer? She had said her husband was dead before his body was found.

"It was Vince who put the idea in my head," said the distraught woman. "When he got into the car in Fernie that night he leaned over to me in the front seat and whispered 'He's dead'."

When Fairbairn returned to Fernie with this ominous admission McDonald was waiting to discuss a clue they had so far overlooked — the candy bar wrappers. For Macchione, the consequence would be as devastating as Mrs. Hudock's remark about her husband being dead before his body had been found.

In the police office McDonald pointed out to Fairbairn that while the four electrical workers had seen a blue coupe on the highway, it might have been somebody else's car. But there were the two candy bar wrappers he had picked up at the murder site. While they might have been thrown out of a passing car, two men stepping out of a car to drink beer wouldn't likely eat candy bars. But the children? The Hudock kids!

The officers immediately headed back to Michel. While their mother looked on, the police officers asked the children if Vince had bought them candy on Sunday. Yes, before they got to the railway station he bought them each a candy bar. What did they do with the wrappers? There was a pause while they considered.

"We just threw them on the floor of the car," said the children, unaware they were helping to put a rope around the neck of their father's killer.

They named the brand of candy; the wrappers in the police office matched.

They must have been scuffed out of the car by the men's feet, or blew out when the car door opened.

The investigation had caused the Provincial Police many extra hours of duty and many sleepless nights. But for the jurors there were also some exhausting hours ahead at Macchione's trial, or rather, trials. For seldom in the history of British Columbia was a man tried for his life so many times.

The first trial was at Cranbrook in May 1936. Macchione's defence was simple: "I went to look for Mike and couldn't find him."

The jury found him guilty and he was sentenced to hang in August. On appeal, however, he got a new trial but twelve months later again heard a jury say "guilty." Again he was sentenced to hang.

Another appeal was made and a third trial was ordered, this time at Vernon in the spring of 1938. The jury could not agree and immediately a fresh trial began. Again the jury could not agree.

A fifth trial was ordered but this time with a difference. The deadlock was broken by a new Crown witness, Rudolph Smalik, who said that on the fatal Sunday he had been curling at the Fernie rink and about 4:30 pm, while driving out on the highway, he had passed Macchione in his blue coupe. Mike Hudock was sitting beside him. Smalik knew both men well, and he was sure of the time because he was on his way to a new job and didn't want to be late.

For the third time in his long duel with the law, Vince Macchione heard a jury foreman give the dreaded pronouncement. This time there was no reprieve.

Early on the morning of October 26, 1938, Vince Macchione, the "good friend" of the Hudock family, stood on the scaffold at Oakalla Prison — then knew no more.

Mystery of the Storekeeper's False Teeth

As rookie policeman Stan Raybone probed the ashes he became convinced that murder was involved. His superiors disagreed — until a Cariboo night two years later.

Nighttime, veteran policemen agree, isn't only the domain of bats and owls. In the city, for instance, there often comes a moment when the boredom of checking buildings, or "shaking hands with doorknobs," is broken by the sudden tinkle of broken glass, the scream of somebody robbed, or knifed, or worse. There are those nights when radio calls crackle in sudden emergency, road blocks are hastily formed and, on occasion, shots exchanged. By contrast, in the country where there might be nobody for miles, a night patrol or vigil can, for an entirely different reason, stimulate the heartbeat.

One of the strangest nighttime episodes that ended in revealing the key to a mystery was told to me many years ago by Stan Raybone, then a Sergeant in the B.C. Provincial Police at Chilliwack, and a thirty-one-year veteran of the force.

In mid-October 1931 while he was stationed at Williams Lake the police got word of a disastrous fire at Forest Grove, a sparsely settled ranching community on the Canim Lake Road not far from 100-Mile House. The District Sergeant being absent at the time, Raybone headed for the scene, somewhat apprehensively since he was a rookie.

Raybone learned when he got there that the blaze had destroyed a combined store and upstairs dwelling operated by S. D. Hoy. For the previous two weeks Hoy's eighty-one-year-old father had been staying with him and both men had perished in the blazing building.

Constable Raybone reported the fire to Kamloops Divisional Headquarters. By chance, a Sergeant of the Criminal Investigation Branch happened to be on the Cariboo Road and was deployed to handle the in-

While stationed at Williams Lake, above in the 1920s, Constable Stan Raybone began a fire investigation which had a startling conclusion.

vestigation. Young Raybone watched the expert with close attention. At the end of a day's probing and questioning it was the Sergeant's conclusion the fire had been accidental, probably due to an over-heated flue. The two men, sound asleep upstairs, had succumbed without warning.

"There was an inquest, of course," Stan told me, "with just enough of the charred remains to identify two male bodies. The upshot was a verdict of accidental death."

The CID Sergeant departed, leaving Raybone to see that the remains, boxed up for shipment to Vancouver and burial, were sent down on the next Pacific Great Eastern train. But since the southbound train was not due for about fourteen hours, the young Constable thought he would pass the time taking a second look at the scene of the fire.

"I was just aimlessly poking around among the charred embers," he told me, "when without thinking of anything in particular I nudged aside some blackened cans with my foot . . . and made a discovery. Under the cans were what I took to be white beans, and when I stooped to examine them I found they were false teeth, about half a dozen of them.

"The plate must have melted, but anyway I picked them up and began to try and figure in my mind how they got there. False teeth are either in a man's mouth or near him when he goes to bed, and I knew that the bedroom, judging by where an iron bedstead had come through the ceiling, was at the other end of the building.

"Then when I started to figure the thing a little closer," he went on, "I noticed there seemed to be a whole row of these blackened cans . . . must have been where the shelving in the store collapsed. So the owner of the teeth must have been down in the store when the fire broke out. Why didn't he rush out into the road? Or did he dash upstairs to rescue his companion?

"Still, the fact that he'd been parted from his teeth didn't make sense. Then I began to get the sneaking notion that there might have been foul

57

play! The more I thought of it, the more I got impressed. Finally, I screwed up my courage, and busting all the conventional channels of communication, sent a wire to the Officer Commanding, giving my suspicions. Back came a wire, precise in instruction, lofty in content. It just said, 'Carry out Sergeant X's instructions'. This order meant ship the bodies, and shut up."

Raybone grinned at the recollection.

"What then?" I enquired.

"Well, there was something else that I learned that got me mystified. I heard the two old men were mighty fond of their big black Labrador dog, but there didn't seem to be any trace of his bones in the fire, and if it had escaped the fire he should have been around. Anyway, it was never seen again."

"A couple of years later," he went on, "when I was still at Williams Lake, one night in early November the phone rang. It was an elderly rancher called Johnson, phoning from a neighbor's place not far out of town.

" 'You'd better come out here right away,' he said. 'I'm at the old Burns' place, and we're in terrible danger. . . .'

"He mumbled something else I couldn't make out, then hung up. But I could tell by his voice that the old boy was scared stiff. So Don Stewart and I jumped in the car and headed for the old Burns' place.

"It was about midnight when we reached the ranch, cloudy and no moon, and blacker'n the inside of a wolf. When we got in sight of the old, weather-beaten ranch house standing there on a slight rise, gaunt and lonely, there wasn't a light to be seen. Then, just where the road took a curve through a poplar windbreak, we suddenly spotted in the car headlights the figure of a man lying face down on the road.

"We hopped out of the car," continued Stan, "and I remember thinking, as we went over to him, that there might have been some sort of wild party. Maybe this was one of the guests who'd passed out. It's an old Cariboo custom.

"When we bent down and turned him over, we saw the party had been rougher than we thought. He was dead! The back of his head was blown out, and beside him lay a .303 Savage rifle.

"It was just a few more steps to the house," continued the Sergeant, "and I used my flash to find the front door, then started pounding on the panels. We waited quite a while before finally there was a glimmer of light inside and pretty soon the door opened, just a crack, and behind it was the face of an old man holding up a lamp.

"It was a creepy sensation," said Stan, with a grin, "to hear those slow shuffling feet, then this startled, withered-looking face in the yellow light of the lamp. I noticed his hand was shaking, maybe with fright, but when he saw the uniform he sort of cooled down.

"He beckoned us silently in, and closing the door after us, led the way into a front room where he slowly put the light on a table. I don't think a word was said.

"Then I noticed a couple of women, one with white hair, sitting on a horsehair sofa. At least one was. The other, much younger and not bad looking, seemed to be sitting on the floor, her head resting against the old lady's knee. The young one had her eyes closed and the old lady kept stroking her hair, and making some sort of crooning noise.

"There was something remarkably queer and eerie about the whole business, and something funny, too, about that young woman. I took a closer look and saw the reason — she was dead, too!

"Then the old man told us the story," he went on. "Seems that his son-in-law, Lawrence Roberts, was a useless type, insanely jealous about his wife, and with a tendency to tilt his arm on occasion. He'd been in to Williams Lake that afternoon and just after dusk, while the Johnsons and their daughter awaited his return, came a rifle shot from outside, and young Mrs. Roberts stumbled and fell to the floor. The bullet had come through one of the living room windows and she was dead in a few minutes.

"The terror-stricken parents," went on Stan, "thinking at any moment they'd be the next target, hastily blew out the lights and, leaving the dead girl on the floor, took off through the back door. Clinging pitifully to one another, and stumbling in the dark, they made their way by a back trail to the Stafford's place, where they phoned the police.

"When they finished their story," continued Raybone, "we asked them who was the dead man lying out on the road.

" 'Dead man? On the road?' Old Johnson was mystified. 'They didn't know of any dead man.'

"So we all went out to take a look and it was then by lantern light that the couple identified their son-in-law, Lawrence Roberts. Appears he had shot himself while they were at the Staffords and they hadn't heard the second, suicide shot."

In daylight the police traced his tracks and found where he'd stood near a fence. Here he watched the flittering lamp-lit figures in the house until he could aim at his wife and kill her. Alongside his tracks was an empty .303 cartridge.

By the time Stan Raybone's story was finished it occurred to me we'd got away from Forest Grove and two old men who were burned up in a grocery store fire. I said as much.

He smiled at me and went on: "When we got the two bodies in to Williams Lake that evening, and searched Robert's clothing what do you think we found?

"A note in his pocket," he went on, after a pause, "confessing to the murder of the two old men at Forest Grove. One of them had been killed down in the store, then packed up to the bedroom. Which explained how his teeth were downstairs! After that he robbed the store, then set it on fire!"

There was a pause.

"Queer to think," he said finally, "that the finale to the mystery of the storekeeper's false teeth would be found two years later in a dead man's pocket."

Well, as I mentioned at the beginning, policemen face many odd — and often scary — situations in the dark of the night.

Tragedy Stalked the Silver Trail

It is doubtful if the B.C. Provincial Police were involved in a more tragic venture than the Eureka Mine on Silver Mountain in the Fraser Valley.

It wasn't by chance that in the summer of 1920 prospector and outdoorsman A. S. Williamson found himself at the entrance to an abandoned mine shaft on a mountain 8 miles (13 km) south of Hope in the Fraser River Valley. In the depths of the cavern, standing ankle deep in ice cold seepage, he noted by the light of his flickering candle that miners had cut their names in a timber, names like "Frenchy," "McEvoy," and "Ned Atkins."

For years Williamson had been hearing scraps of gossip from Indians about a lost mine in the Hope Mountains and that summer of 1920 he decid-

ed to look for it. He said nothing to anyone, and took a rifle to give the impression he was going hunting.

After following the east bank of Silver Creek for several miles he headed on an old trail up Eureka Creek. At one point he noticed an old horse corral and, near timberline, the remains of an ancient log cabin with a huge fireplace and an assay outfit.

Higher and higher he climbed around the shoulders of Silver Peak, until he came to a narrow ravine and the remains of a blacksmith's shop. The bottom of the ravine was filled with hardened snow but near an overhanging rock wall was a crevasse between the rock and snow. He climbed down, and on hands and knees entered a tunnel.

Cautiously moving forward, he felt under the water some wooden

The Eureka Mine in the 1870s and, inset, "Happy" Tom Schooley and his young bride before tragedy struck in 1872.

tracks and slowly followed them. They led to a wooden ore car with iron wheels. It seemed as good as new. Tools were scattered around as if men had just quit work, instead of nearly half a century before, and here and there candles were stuck in the lagging.

Although he didn't know at the time, Williamson had re-discovered B.C.'s first quartz mine, the ill-fated Eureka (or Eureka-Victoria as it was later known) where nothing had been touched since 1875. There were some other events connected with the mine and its original owners that Williamson also didn't know. How the mine brought nothing but tragedy to the five people first involved — "Happy Tom" Schooley, for instance, who met the hangman, and pioneer B.C. sawmill owner Sewell Prescott "Sue" Moody who drowned when the *Pacific* foundered off Victoria with the loss of all the nearly 300 on board.

The story began in Yale in the summer of 1868 when Indian Peter Emery returned from a hunting trip in the mountains to show his friend Tom Schooley a sample of silver ore he'd picked up. It was rich stuff. Fabulously rich.

Schooley, a miner, knew ore. He'd crossed the American plains with a wagon train to become a Forty-niner in California, then headed north to Victoria in 1858 for the Fraser River rush. He'd seen Yale spring from a simple trading post to a wild community of honkytonks and saloons. Tall, dark and handsome, always distinguished by his white cowboy hat, Tom Schooley was the life of every gathering, and for that reason was dubbed "Happy Tom."

The rock Pete Emery offered him was an exciting find. For it he gave Pete a rifle, and made a coffin for Pete's wife who had just died. The coffin was a portent of what was to follow.

Schooley climbed Silver Peak and promptly recognized the ore as one of the richest silver finds in the country. Instead of staking claims, however, he got a Crown grant to three lots, then went looking for partners.

He didn't have far to go. First he interested George Deitz, an old buddy of the original Fraser River rush who, backed by Wells Fargo money, was now running a prosperous stage line between Yale and the Cariboo. Another Fraser River original who put up money was S. P. "Sue" Moody, founder of the sawmill community of Moodyville on the north shore of Burrard Inlet.

In Victoria, Schooley sparked Frank Garesche's interest. Garesche, a former Wells Fargo employee in San Francisco, was in business for himself running a private bank. The fourth man was Henry Forman, a one-time Victoria alderman, who was to become Schooley's father-in-law.

With this backing the Eureka Mining Company was formed and soon 3,000, $50 shares were bought up. After Schooley's block of shares was sold his status changed from that of an ordinary miner to a well-to-do promoter. Then, after a whirlwind courtship, he married the beautiful Ellen Forman.

Unfortunately, trouble arose soon after their San Francisco honeymoon when Happy Tom surprisingly turned into Surly Tom. Some say he was insanely jealous of his wife, others say he suspected his father-in-law of having designs on his money. More likely, Schooley's bad business judg-

When the *Pacific* sank in November 1875 off Vancouver Island all of her nearly 300 passengers and crew were drowned. Among those on board were S.P. Moody, top left, and F. Garesche, two of the original partners in the Eureka Mine. Also drowned was Provincial Police Superintendent J.H. Sullivan, top right, who had supervised Tom Schooley's hanging.

ment was the cause. Tom started out as if he had all the money in the world, but a succession of unwise investments dwindled his funds. He became increasingly surly and suspicious, seeking more and more consolation from the bottle. Finally, in January 1874 when he and his wife and two-month-old daughter were staying with the Formans, tragedy enveloped the family.

Tom had been drinking steadily all day, getting more ill-tempered by the hour. That afternoon he threatened his wife with violence, and smashed some of the furniture. Finally, at the dinner table Henry Forman took such exception to his son-in-law's attitude that he picked up his plate and went into the kitchen to eat alone.

Schooley, an ugly look in his eye, staggered after him. Lounging in the doorway, he produced a revolver.

Forman's fork was half way to his mouth when Schooley fired. The bullet pierced Forman's hand, gouged the table and bounced into the wall. Forman jumped up and ran to the back door. As he reached it another bullet ploughed into his back. With a gasp he wrenched open the door and stumbled out. His wife and Ellen ran to help and summoned the doctor and police.

Dr. J. S. Helmcken's diagnosis was a gloomy one. He doubted that Forman would live through the night. Police Inspector Bloomfield, accompanied by Constables Clark, Beech and McPhee and the police magistrate, took the dying man's declaration then turned his attention to the Forman house.

Schooley had locked all the doors. However, a knife blade under a kitchen window gained them entry. With the aid of their bull's eye lamps, the squad searched the house. They found Schooley, lying on his back on the floor, dead drunk, a two-gallon jug of port wine beside him, a loaded revolver in his hand. Another cocked and loaded revolver lay beside him on the floor and in his pocket he had two loaded derringers. Schooley was soon disarmed and on his way to jail.

Next morning Forman died and Schooley was charged with murder. It was now Penitent Tom who came up at the March Assize to face a bench of judges that included Chief Justice Matthew Baillie Begbie, H. P. P. Crease and J. Hamilton Gray.

Rocke Robertson did his best for the defence, stressing that it wasn't a crime of revenge, but a killing without malice aforethought. He spoke of Schooley's previous good character, his happy disposition and called for a verdict of manslaughter "prompted by the dictates of mercy."

"One man has died," he said to the jury. "Don't add to the crime and make it two deaths."

The jury took a mere twenty minutes to find Schooley guilty. When he was asked if he had anything to say before being sentenced, Happy Tom took the opportunity of explaining that he purchased the derringers years before in San Francisco in anticipation of a trip to Nevada where "the highwaymen were reported active on the stage road."

Justice Gray, referring to this statement, noted: "No man requires to move about this community with firearms on his person; no man need carry a revolver or the life of another human being in his pocket. No stranger commentary than your remarks could be produced and if men act as you have done they will find that British law will drag down the highest that may dare to break it as it will lift up and protect the humblest who has been trampled underfoot. . . . Let the fate of this prisoner be a warning to men who carry firearms in any part of the province; they will be taught that when men take life they will be hanged as sure as there is a God in heaven!''

Schooley found himself with just two months to live. On a morning in late May he rose from his prison cot to take his last look at the blue sky and fleecy clouds. By 7.30 a.m. the roofs of buildings overlooking the jail yard were crowded with sightseers — people in holiday mood, jocular and friendly.

Inside the fence of the prison yard was a smaller crowd, invited in by a guard who swung the gate open. As the crowd waited, the masked executioner was in Schooley's cell, pinioning his arms with a leather belt. Provincial Police Superintendent John H. Sullivan nodded to a guard and the cell door opened. A few minutes later Happy Tom was no more.

That fall, in November, two more Eureka shareholders met death. Frank Garesche and S. P. Moody, hoping to interest San Francisco capital in the Eureka Mine, took passage on the steamer *Pacific*, which collided with a sailing ship off Cape Flattery. Among those drowned were Garesche and Moody, and Provincial Police Superintendent Sullivan who had supervised Schooley's hanging.

With four of its chief promotors dead, the Eureka didn't survive long, despite exceptional assay reports revealed in old records of the B.C. Department of Mines. With silver selling at $1.10 an ounce, the first shipment of ore assayed $460 a ton "with thousands of tons of rock in sight." Once, two mules brought down a load that yielded 750 ounces of silver bullion.

The first annual report of the Mines Department in 1874 mentions a seam at the Eureka "four to seven feet in width, traced for 3,000 feet . . . the ore assaying from $20 to $1,050 a ton." The richer Van Bremner lead on the same property had run up to $2,400 a ton. Despite these glowing reports, it was still a difficult task to bring out the ore. Finally, dissension among the owners caused a shutdown, and the stock slumped.

Maybe this unexpected financial setback mentally unbalanced the remaining original shareholder, George Dietz. Not long after, his wife made a court application to have his affairs taken out of his hands. Without recovering, George died in California at 54.

In this aura of tragedy, for the next forty-five years the Eureka workings remained silent until the summer day in 1920 when A. S. Williamson re-discovered the mine. Acting as agent for Sperry and White in Seattle, he picked up the property in a tax sale. Plans were made to re-open the mine. Records show, however, that nothing much happened. In 1935, the Mines Department record ends laconically with "Struck off."

B.C.'s first quartz mine had become just another hole in the ground, but not before tragically affecting the lives of its five promoters.

In February 1915 "Chubby" Clinger rode
confidently into Clinton, murdered partner's money
in his pocket, alibi polished. Unfortunately,
District Chief Frank Aiken quickly solved

The Case of the Frozen Corpse

Albert Lester "Chubby" Clinger and Betty Coward saw each other for only a moment as they passed in the hallway of the Clinton Courthouse in
1915. But somehow it seemed appropriate that fate should have directed
their paths together. They had much in common. Both were Americans,
and both had left California in 1914 to homestead in British Columbia.
Although they settled 120 miles (193 km) apart, their parallel course continued. Both had murdered their partners; both concocted an alibi to out-
wit justice; both lost because of brilliant work by two policemen.

Chubby Clinger's story opened in the early spring of 1915. The vast
plateau of the Cariboo rangeland still lay under a mantle of snow as he
rode into Clinton for supplies one February afternoon. Chubby was fairly
well known in the district and as he lolled large and comfortable on his
ambling cayuse, he exchanged greetings with some of the Monday afternoon idlers.

Clinger, who was short and fat, had arrived from California the
previous year with a partner, lean and lanky Thomas Burton Smith. The
partners were not only dissimilar physically but also in personality. Smith
was quiet while Chubby talked to everybody. The pair finally took up a
pre-emption at Springhouse Prairie, about 45 miles (73 km) northwest of
Clinton. It was good grazing country and with their stock they felt
confident of success, especially with the war in Europe and rising beef prices.

Smith didn't often come to Clinton, so it was Clinger who usually rode
into town to buy supplies. This particular afternoon Chubby was crossing
the road to the Clinton Hotel for a drink when he met Frank Aiken, 35-year-
old District Chief of the B.C. Provincial Police.

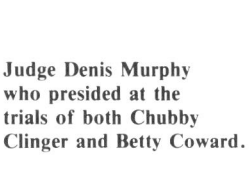

Chubby Clinger was crossing the
road to the Clinton Hotel, above in
the 1890s, when he met B.C. Policeman
Frank Aiken and reported that his
partner had robbed him.

Judge Denis Murphy
who presided at the
trials of both Chubby
Clinger and Betty Coward.

"Frank, you're just the man I want to see," was Chubby's breezy greeting. "Can we go over to your office and have a talk?"

A few minutes later in the modest wooden police station, Chubby unburdened himself of a story. Seems, as so often happens, the Clinger-Smith partnership had dissolved with extraordinary suddenness. It happened one night when he and Smith were camped on the Dog Creek Trail on the way out from Springhouse to Ashcroft to buy some equipment. When morning dawned Clinger was surprised to find that both Smith and his horse had gone — along with $200 from Chubby's pocket.

"Can you imagine that dirty son-of-a-bitch," Chubby fumed, trying to roll a Bull Durham cigarette in his nervous excitement. "Jack-rolling his partner? I wouldn't have thought it possible. No, sir, I wouldn't have thought it possible."

"Did you try to follow him?" asked Aiken.

"Sure, I checked his tracks," said Chubby, "followed them for a couple of miles, then lost them when I found myself down in some cattle-beaten hay meadow and couldn't pick them up again."

"Well . . . it don't matter anyway," he continued. "I don't care if I never see him again." He paused to suck his cigarette, then added, "And I guess nobody else around here will.

"I'd had the idea for some time that he was going to pull out and leave me. Now and again in the past month he spoke of leaving and going to Romania."

"Romania?" echoed the puzzled policeman.

"Yeah. He's got a boy there, working for the Standard Oil Company, and he said once or twice he'd like to go to Europe and join him."

The interview ended with Aiken taking a signed statement from Chubby.

After Chubby left, Aiken sat in thought. Then he got up and cranked the handle of the wall phone to contact Constable Jack Bourne at 150 Mile House, the next police post on the Cariboo Road, 100 miles (160 km) north of Clinton.

Aiken merely asked him to report at Clinton as soon as possible. When Bourne cantered in to Clinton the next evening, he briefed him on Chubby Clinger's story, and finally remarked: "You know, Bourne, there's something fishy about that yarn. For one thing, he didn't seem particularly interested in getting his money back. That 'good riddance to bad rubbish' line doesn't sound right."

"You think he's trying to put something over on Smith and using the police?" asked Bourne.

"I don't know what to think," said Aiken. "But I know if it had been anyone else they would have been madder'n hell, and yelling for the police to get their money back."

He lit his pipe, then added: "And this story about Smith heading for Romania. With the war on and all that, how would he ever get to Romania? If he was leaving the country with money he stole he wouldn't get past Ashcroft without being seen."

Aiken's reasoning was based on the sound knowledge that no one goes unnoticed where the population is scarce. In cattle country everything about

Until about 1916 convicted murderers from Interior B.C. were hanged at Kamloops. Clinger, however, was probably the last man hanged at the jail, above, since convicted murderers were afterward taken to the Lower Mainland for execution.

a passing stranger was observed, from the age of his horse to the color of his shirt.

"Well, anyway," said Aiken, "I feel that you and I better get on the trail of Mr. Smith and try to get Chubby's money back."

Next day, trailing a packhorse, they wended their way over the snow-covered and barely evident rangeland trails until they arrived at Springhouse Prairie where they found the Smith-Clinger homestead deserted. After examining the little log cabin, Aiken — considered one of the best bushmen the Cariboo had known — and Bourne rode round the homestead. They finally picked up signs of two riders who, by the history of the weather, had ridden off about a week ago. The track led in the direction of the partners' nearest neighbor, Napoleon Pigeon, who lived some 25 miles (40 km) away.

For miles the two police officers jogged along until the light of the early spring afternoon waned and they reined in where the tracks seemed to end. Dismounting, they examined the ground. In a brush-screened draw they found the body of a man. Aiken recognized him as Tom Smith, frozen stiff. Cause of death was readily apparent — a bullet hole in the back of his head. Smith had been murdered.

Aiken found nothing of value in the dead man's pockets. The next morning he and Bourne searched the immediate area but found nothing. There was no sign of a struggle or of the murdered man's horse. Aiken concluded that if it had not been led away by the murderer, it must have wandered in search of food.

69

The evidence suggested that Smith had been shot as he knelt by the fire. The bullet had penetrated the unfortunate man's skull from back to front and was lost somewhere in the undergrowth. From the bullet's obvious velocity it was fired from a rifle.

Lashing Smith's body on the packhorse the two policemen headed back to Clinton, arriving two days later. Chubby Clinger was still there, grumbling about his partner's deceit. He was astonished to learn that Smith had been found dead.

"Must have been some Indian who caught up with him," was his gloomy surmise.

An autopsy was held on February 14 on the murdered Smith. Next day (just a week after Chubby had ridden in to Clinton to report his partner's disappearance) Dr. Sanson, the coroner, held an inquest. The six-man jury heard the police and medical evidence, as well as Chubby's tale of his partner's perfidy. The rangeland jury came to the conclusion that Smith had been murdered by his partner, Chubby Clinger.

Later that day, as the remains of Smith were being buried, a chastened Clinger peered through the cell bars in the Clinton lockup. Across the hall in his office, Aiken reviewed the case. True, the dead man had no money in his pockets while Chubby had close to $100 when he was arrested. But that didn't prove it was Smith's money.

On the chance that some cowpuncher, rancher or Indian had seen the pair together about the time of Smith's death, Aiken next day left for Dog Creek. His travels finally took him to the Pigeon Ranch — and some interesting information.

Rancher Pigeon mentioned that he had recently received a letter from the murdered Smith, saying that he was leaving the country, possibly going to Europe. As he had to leave in a hurry, Smith wrote that he was sorry there was no time for a personal goodbye. "Funny he should write to me like that," Pigeon concluded, "because we never saw much of one another."

After studying the letter, Aiken tucked it in his notebook. Then he left, but as he rode back to Clinton couldn't help thinking that money might have been the motive for the crime. He wondered whether Smith had a bank account and, if so, where? There was only one way to find out. He headed his horse in the direction of the cabin on Springhouse Prairie. There he searched until he found what he wanted — some of Smith's returned cheques from the Bank of British North America at Ashcroft. These, too, he tucked in his notebook since they provided samples of Smith's signature.

When he got back to his Clinton office, Aiken telephoned Chief Constable Colin Cameron at Ashcroft. He would like Cameron to check with the Bank to see what funds were in Smith's account and if there were any cancelled cheques. Within an hour Cameron reported that Smith had about $1,000 in his account and there were several cancelled cheques.

"What was the date of the last cheque that Smith issued?" Aiken asked.

"February 11," said Cameron.

"The 11th! Are you sure?"

"Absolutely," said Cameron. "I'm in the bank now and I've got the cancelled cheque in my hand."

"But good heavens," went on Aiken, "that was the day we found his body . . . and he'd already been dead a week." Then he hastily added, "You'd better let me have that cheque. It's going to be valuable."

Two days later with the cheque in his hand, and strong suspicion in his mind, Aiken spread on his desk the letter that Pigeon had received, the cancelled cheques found in Smith's cabin, the cheque returned from Ashcroft, and a sample of Clinger's handwriting in a letter from the local government agent's files. As he studied the writing and the signatures a picture formed. Clinger had penned the letter that Pigeon thought was from Smith and forged Smith's name to a cheque for $57 on February 11, the day the policemen found Smith's frozen body in the brush-covered gully.

After a preliminary hearing Clinger was committed for trial, but the case was set over until the Fall Assize because Constable Jack Bourne was in hospital. He had been badly cut by flying glass when he retrieved a prisoner who made a leap for liberty through the window of a Pacific Great Eastern Railway train near Squamish.

Thus it was in September that Mr. Justice Denis Murphy mounted the bench in the Clinton Assize Court. The witnesses were heard, and finally Clinger took the witness stand to tell again how he had been robbed by Smith as he lay wrapped in his blankets by a Cariboo camp fire. This time, however, he changed the sequel. He said he had trailed Smith for miles and finally caught up with him. He was going to hail his thieving partner at rifle point, but suddenly he stumbled on a snow-covered log and the gun went off accidentally, killing Smith.

"I got my money back, but I was scared to death. So scared that I didn't dare tell the real story to the police. That's why I told Chief Aiken that I lost Smith's tracks in the snow."

In his summing up, Judge Murphy pointed out to the jury that Clinger stated he was dazed and stupefied after the shooting, "a point he contradicted by the deliberate manner in which he said he got the money off the corpse."

The twelve cattle country jurymen, wise to rangeland habits and ways, were also wise to human frailty and cupidity. They were out forty-five minutes and returned with a verdict of "Guilty."

The pudgy little man from California, his face now drawn and grey, stood up long enough to hear Judge Murphy tell him that he had ninety days to live. He would hang at the Kamloops jail on December 23, 1915.

Clinger turned at the touch of a policeman's hand on his arm and shuffled back to his cell. On the way down the corridor he had to stand aside as another police officer and a matron escorted a small, dark-haired woman toward the court room.

She was Betty Coward whose life, as already mentioned, for the past year had paralleled that of Chubby Clinger's. As related in the next chapter, she was also being tried for murder and before the same judge. Although Chubby didn't know it at the time, he'd had a momentary glimpse of the first woman to be sentenced to death by hanging in British Columbia.

She Shot Her Way to a Death Sentence

She insisted that an Indian had murdered her husband. But District Chief W.R. Dunwoody was suspicious and followed a series of clues several thousand miles to a surprise conclusion.

"Lucetta, Lucetta, there's someone at the door!"

It was about 10 o'clock on the night of September 6, 1915, near Fort St. James in Central B.C. Inside an isolated log cabin on their homestead slept two women — Florence Whitehouse and Lucetta McInnes. The startled Lucetta, now fully awake, also heard the banging on the cabin door and the anguished cries of a woman. Hastily lighting an oil lamp, the women opened the door. Two figures, clad in night attire, stumbled in. They were the wife and stepdaughter of a nearby homesteader. Hysterically, they told an incoherent story of death and a family tragedy.

The women who opened the door to the frightened nighttime visitors were also homesteaders. They were part of an influx of settlers resulting from the completion of the Grand Trunk Pacific Railway the previous year across Central B.C. to a new Pacific port called Prince Rupert. Their cabin was 5 miles (8 km) from the historic trading settlement of Fort St. James at the foot of Stuart Lake. Another 25 miles (40 km) south on the wagon road lay the village of Vanderhoof on the new railway.

Near to the Whitehouse-McInnes cabin was the makeshift habitation of the Cowards, Jim and Elizabeth. It was 40-year-old Betty and her 17-year-old daughter, Rose, who had suddenly made their appearance.

When the two unexpected visitors were able to give a rational account of what had happened, the spinster settlers were shocked to learn that Jim Coward had apparently been murdered in his sleep. Mrs. Coward, in her fear-stricken account, repeatedly mentioned something about an Indian with

District Chief W.R. Dunwoody, and the Clinton Courthouse where in 1915 both Chubby Clinger and Elizabeth Coward were convicted.

a grudge. The Coward women, too nervous to return to their cabin, spent the night with the two women. In the morning all four mustered courage to go over the bush trail to the Coward's cabin.

There they viewed Jim Coward, cold in death, lying on a makeshift outdoor bed. At the sight of his body, Betty Coward gave a heart-rending cry and fell down beside the bed, clutching her husband. When she calmed down they found a neighbor who rode into Vanderhoof to flash a telegram to Provincial Police District Chief W. R. Dunwoody at Fort George, 75 miles (120 km) to the east.

Thirty-six-year-old Bill Dunwoody, once a member of the famous Royal Irish Constabulary, had two attributes useful in a policeman — tireless energy and a sense of humor, qualities that were to carry him to the post of Deputy Commissioner.

In due course Dunwoody swung off the train at Vanderhoof with Constable Rupert W. Rayner and onto a horse-drawn rig that held coroner D. B. Lazier, Justice of the Peace Dave Hoy, and Dr. W. D. Stone.

When they arrived at the lonely Coward cabin and viewed the body, Dunwoody took the usual statement from Betty Coward. As he did so, he noted that she was a small, dark-haired woman whose swarthy complexion gave hint of Latin blood.

From Mrs. Coward's statement Dunwoody learned, among other things, that the couple had come from the United States the year before to take up their pre-emption. Rose Dell, Mrs. Coward's daughter by a former marriage, had joined them later. Like most pre-emptors, they found much to do, a situation that explained their makeshift cabin with its sheet iron heater which also served as a stove, and the two rough wooden bunks.

When daughter Rose joined them, explained Betty Coward, Jim Coward slept outdoors in a bed made up in the body of a sleigh. Apparently there was no ill-feeling in the family and on the night of Coward's death when he left for his outdoor bunk, his wife and stepdaughter made ready for bed in the cabin. They were in their bunks, the light out, stated Mrs. Coward, when she heard a sudden shout and a shot. Hastily re-lighting the lamp, she and Rose rushed out to the sleigh and, to their horror, found Coward dead. Mrs. Coward again voiced the opinion that the killing was the work of a Vanderhoof Indian with whom Coward had had an argument about the price of transporting a trunk from the railroad station to the cabin.

Dunwoody and the doctor next turned their attention to the dead man, and found themselves a little mystified.

Coward lay on his back, the bedclothes practically undisturbed, an old piece of tarpaulin over the blankets as protection from the early morning dew or frost. The mosquito netting which had covered his face had been pulled aside, and he had been shot, but in strange fashion. The bullet had entered one nostril and so close had been the muzzle that his moustache and eyebrows were singed. His right arm lay out of the bunk and on the ground was a .32 calibre Ivor-Johnson revolver which had recently been discharged.

Dr. Stone was of the opinion that death had been instantaneous. Dunwoody, remembering Mrs. Coward's account of a shout and a shot, wondered who had shouted. Surely not her husband; and if the murderer had shouted then Coward would naturally have been awakened. It was an interesting problem.

Rather than further distress the already over-wrought wife and daughter, Dunwoody arranged for their transportation to Vanderhoof. When they had gone Dr. Stone performed an autopsy, recovering the fatal bullet from Coward's brain. Dunwoody washed the slightly deformed slug and, as he contemplatively handled it, came to an interesting conclusion. By its weight it was more like a .38 than a .32-calibre bullet.

After Coward's remains were prepared for the widow's final instructions, Dunwoody made his way to the cabin of Lucetta McInnes and Florence Whitehouse. There, over a cup of tea, suspicion began to form in his mind. The women settlers, reciting the events of the tragic evening, said that Mrs. Coward had told them that she was about to go to bed when she heard the shot. She had told Dunwoody she was already in bed. A small matter, but still . . .?

Back in Vanderhoof before the inquest was held, Dunwoody searched out the Indian suspect named by Betty Coward. It took him less than an hour to discover that the Indian had nothing to do with Coward's death. He had been continually in the company of white men in Vanderhoof from dusk to midnight on the night of the tragedy.

After the inquest the jury returned an open verdict: Jim Coward had been murdered by a person or persons unknown.

During the proceedings there was one thing that didn't escape the vigilant Dunwoody's notice. When Mrs. Coward gave her evidence, this time she elaborated a little. She said she was in her nightdress, kneeling by her bunk saying her prayers when she heard the shot. It was a touch of color that strengthened Dunwoody's distrust of her story.

At the inquest he had given evidence that the bullet that took Coward's life was fired from a .38 caliber revolver. He was sure of this because he borrowed a pair of gold scales from the local Hudson's Bay manager and compared the weight of the fatal bullet with half a dozen others pulled from new .38 shells. Although the fatal bullet was slightly deformed, it hadn't lost weight.

"There must be a gun somewhere," was the overpowering thought in Dunwoody's mind. To find it he went back the next day to the Coward cabin with Constable Rayner and Dave Hoy. Although they made a thorough search of the building's interior they failed to find any trace of a weapon. Rayner, however, discovered the next best thing — a cartridge belt filled with .38 shells.

Then a loose board in a corner of the floor caused Dunwoody to pause. He lifted it. Underneath was a small, leather bound notebook, evidently the property of the dead man. The last entry read: "Threatened to shoot me if I molested the dog in any way. This was about 7 a.m. September 2, 1915."

It would be ironic, thought Dunwoody, if four days before his murder the dead man had inadvertently put a rope around the killer's neck! But the entry made this much clear. Suspicion centered on two people: Betty Coward and her daughter, Rose.

His ruminations were cut short by a shout from Dave Hoy who had been poking around outside the cabin. At the side of the house idle curiosity prompted him to lift the edge of a galvanized washtub lying upside down on the ground. Underneath it was the object of Dunwoody's search — a .38 revolver.

It was fully loaded except for one empty cartridge. After he examined it, Dunwoody placed it carefully back under the tub with the quiet observation, "I think we'll just leave it there." The discovery had prompted an idea.

Next day in Vanderhoof, Dunwoody was approached by Betty Coward who asked if it was all right to go back to the cabin and pick up some of her belongings. She did not plan to live there. In fact, she added, she and her daughter were returning to the States.

Dunwoody, helpful and sympathetic, immediately arranged for her to use Dave Hoy's rig. As soon as she was out of sight, he had some terse instructions for Constable Rayner. "Saddle up and get back to that cabin as quick as you can. Get there before she arrives and post yourself where she can't see you. Be sure to keep out of sight, but above all keep your eye on that washtub."

Minutes later Rayner nonchalantly cantered out of the community on a bush trail, but once beyond the settlement broke into a gallop. He hobbled his horse a short distance from the cabin, then stealthily approached the deserted building. For a hiding place he settled on a makeshift barn. Through cracks in the rough vertical siding he could keep the washtub in view, as well as the cabin door.

Two hours passed before a horse-drawn rig approached. When it stopped, he heard the voice of Betty Coward and Lucetta McInnes. Mrs. Coward, obviously not wishing to return to the murder scene alone, had asked Lucetta to keep her company. The women entered the cabin and ten minutes later he saw them emerge, each with an armful of clothing. Then he heard Mrs. Coward remark, "You take these things, Lucetta, and put them in the rig. I've got to go back and pick up something I've forgotten. I won't be a minute."

As the laden Lucetta walked round the side of the building, Rayner saw Mrs. Coward stand for a second or two in the cabin's doorway. When sure that her companion was out of sight, she stepped out and hastily made for the washtub. She tilted it up on edge. Then, satisfied with what she saw, dropped it in position again.

When the women drove off, Rayner picked up the hidden gun and headed back to Vanderhoof to make his report. The Constable's story was enough for Dunwoody. Promptly he arrested Betty Coward for the murder of her husband, and Rose Dell as an accessory.

It was now September 9 and the Fall Assize at Clinton was scheduled for the first week in October. Dunwoody had less than a month to fill in any gaps in the Coward case, to learn the real reason for Betty Coward taking her husband's life.

When he returned to his Fort George office, Dunwoody exchanged a series of coded telegrams with his chief in Victoria. That evening he boarded a Grand Trunk Pacific train. It was the start of a journey of thousands of miles, one that would take him through thirteen states and three provinces. It would also give him the answer to a cryptic entry in a dead man's diary.

Once across the U.S. border, Dunwoody headed for San Francisco. Here he checked records and rang door bells until he learned that Mrs. Coward, when she was Mrs. Dell, ran a boarding house. One of her boarders was a 40-year-old bachelor, Jim Coward, a guard at the San Francisco exhibition.

Mrs. Dell, apparently separated from her first husband, had taken a liking to Jim and eventually the couple had gone to Canada to take up land.

Next, Dunwoody visited Watsonville, California, where he finally succeeded in finding her first husband. He learned also that Dell was more than pleased when his wife went off with Coward.

"Went off with her?" queried Dunwoody. "I thought they met for the first time when he boarded with her in San Francisco."

"No. You've got it all wrong," said Dell. "They got acquainted when Coward was town marshal of Forest City, Iowa, where we used to live. They got real chummy, then one morning skipped town together. I heard later they were in San Francisco."

"She's a dangerous woman," said Dell reflectively, "and has a hell of a temper. You mark my words, she'll commit murder one day."

It seemed to Dunwoody, as he took his departure, that that day had already arrived.

Dunwoody next visited Forest City. After a day's search he uncovered another important clue. Elizabeth Dell had insured Coward's life for a considerable sum of money just before the couple left and the premiums had been paid regularly.

Heading north to Winnipeg, Dunwoody interviewed the Grand Trunk Railway land agent who had helped the couple settle at Fort St. James. After satisfying himself he had learned as much as he could, the persistent Police Chief returned to B.C. A few days later, at the Clinton Assize, Betty Coward's defence was shattered by the facts Dunwoody had collected.

Mr. Justice Denis Murphy congratulated the energetic Dunwoody, and the jury quickly found Mrs. Coward guilty.

Judge Murphy, who had just sentenced Chubby Clinger to the gallows for the murder of his partner, now had the grim duty of sentencing another northland pre-empter for the murder of her common-law partner.

When she heard her sentence pronounced in the Clinton courtroom that afternoon, Betty Coward became the first woman to be condemned to death in B.C. The case against Rose Dell was dropped.

Coward was scheduled to die alongside Chubby Clinger at Kamloops jail on December 23, 1915. Forty-eight hours before her appointment with the hangman, however, she had her sentence commuted to life imprisonment.

The first jury couldn't reach a verdict; the second
said "guilty," and he was sentenced to hang; the third
said "not guilty," and he was set free. But for
Karl Fredericks fate had decreed that

Death be not Denied

An old Persian fable involves two rug dealers chatting in a bazaar. One of them suddenly spied Death on the edge of the crowd. "I must go," he said hurriedly to his companion. "I see Death approaching. I think he's looking for me."

"Where will you be safe?" asked his companion.

"In Samara. He'll never find me there."

With that he slipped into the crowd. A moment later Death approached the man who remained. "Your friend disappeared before I could meet him," said Death. Then he added: "But it doesn't matter. I have an appointment with him tomorrow in Samara."

The records of the B.C. Provincial Police reveal that a German immigrant named Karl Fredericks had an experience similar to that of the rug dealer, except that his appointment with Death was not in Samara but in Nazi Germany.

The story opened on a sunny afternoon in late June 1930 in the Central B.C. village of Vanderhoof, gateway to a vast roadless area dotted with rugged peaks and slashed with the water of huge lakes such as Stuart and Takla. In his office Constable H. J. Jennings was having difficulty understanding what tall Anatole Matise of the Tachi Indian band was telling him. It apparently involved a story of suspicion and mystery that was circulating around the fires at Tachi and other Indian settlements.

The Indians had decided to inform the white men of what had happened. From the Tachi River some 50 miles (80 km) to the north the moccasined Anatole had slipped south by canoe until he arrived, smelling of sweat and woodsmoke, in the Vanderhoof police office. Here he related in his halting, monosyllabic style a story that might mean something — or nothing.

From what Constable Jennings could make out, a couple of weeks before three white men with a boatload of supplies had gone up the Tachi River, the link between Stuart Lake and Trembleur Lake. Two days later

Stuart Lake in Central B.C. Here in 1930 Karl Fredericks,
inset, and two companions set out with a boat load of
supplies for Trembleur Lake. Only Fredericks returned.

one of the men returned and at Tachi Indian village walked into the trading post of Cassiar Robert. He looked over the stock on the shelves and appeared to be in a spending mood. The stranger asked the price of a moosehide coat, and when told it was $18 promptly handed over the money. He expressed interest in moccasins and gloves, and when a squaw produced a few pairs of each, bought the lot.

Cassiar Robert noticed the man's .30-30 Winchester and offered to buy it for $20. He wouldn't sell. But to Cassiar's surprise, a few minutes later the stranger swapped the rifle for another Indian's nearly worthless fox pelt. The Indian told him the pelt wasn't of much value but the white man wanted it anyway.

Next the stranger was intrigued with a pair of moose horns hanging on the wall. "There's a cache of food up the river you can have for those horns," he said.

Cassiar was now not only surprised but also puzzled. A food cache can mean the difference between comfort or hardship; life or death. He was reluctant to clinch this deal. What about his partners? Wouldn't they need the food?

The stranger made it plain, however, that the cache was his to dispose of. As proof he wrote a pencilled authority on a slip of paper.

It was hard at times for Constable Jennings to know what Matise was getting at. The rambling story sounded like trading post gossip. But, as the man had come of his own will to tell it, there must be more. Jennings waited patiently.

Matise went on to say that the Indians asked the white man about his two companions. They were told they had gone up the lake with two Indian boys as guides. Why was the stranger heading south? He was sick, he said.

"Where you sick?" one asked suspiciously. The white man pointed to his side. "Pain here," was his only comment.

The Indians were too bush-wise to believe his explanation. They knew that only a healthy man could cover the Tachi Trail in two days, especially while carrying a pack. If his two companions had made a base camp on Trembleur Lake, why hadn't this man, if he was sick, used the boat to return south? And the story about two boys acting as guides was obviously a lie. An important Indian celebration was planned for the next two days and no Indian would go anywhere if it meant missing the event of the year.

When some of the Indians questioned the man's story, he showed signs of nervousness and broke off the conversation. The next day he hired Peter Seymour to take him by boat to Fort St. James where he grabbed his pack and moose horns and beat Seymour down a dollar in the fare. The last Seymour saw of him he was hitching a lift to Vanderhoof in a light delivery truck.

After the stranger's departure the Tachi Indians mulled over the matter around the evening fire. The result was that Anatole Matise was delegated to inform the police at Vanderhoof of the incident and their suspicions. This he had now done, although when it came to describing the three men there was a baffling lack of detail. The best Matise could do was to catalogue the trapping trio as "one big man," " the middle-sized man" and "the little man." The man whom the Indians spoke to in the store was the middle-sized one.

From trap line records and information supplied by a Vanderhoof farmer, George Cameron, Constable Jennings pieced together the trio's identity. A month before they had worked two weeks clearing land for Cameron and were paid $149 by cheque. The "tall man" was Max Westphal, a 6-ft. (183-cm) German Army veteran from World War One. He was described as having a slow walk, an erect bearing, a clean-shaven face, sandy hair, and a porcelain bridge on his upper front teeth.

The "middle-size" man was Karl Fredericks, 28, dark-haired and sallow-faced. He, too, was a German Army veteran and had been in Canada only six months.

Smallest of the three was Herman Peters, about Fredericks age, aggressive, alert and probably leader of the trio. Peters was distinguished by a slight limp and widely spaced good teeth.

From these descriptions it was plain that the man who had returned was Fredericks. A check at the Vanderhoof railway station showed that he had bought a ticket for Edmonton, Alberta. The station agent remembered him because of the moose horns he carried.

"You can't check those as baggage," the agent had warned. "You'll have to send them on by express."

For answer the young man promptly tossed the horns into a nearby clump of brush.

Jennings reported this information to his District Sergeant at Prince George, W. J. "Big Bill" Service. He instructed Jennings to go to Tachi and see what he could find out.

When Jennings searched the southern margin of Trembleur Lake, he found the camp, the boat and a cache of food, but no signs of life. After two days of unsuccessful searching, it was plain to Jennings that any further investigation would have to be undertaken on a bigger scale with proper equipment. As a result, a week later Inspector W. V. E. Spiller arrived from Prince George with Sergeant Service and Constable J. H. McClinton. After a short conference in the little Vanderhoof police office, they headed for Tachi. There they interrogated the Indians, then pushed on to Trembleur Lake.

Spiller and Service criss-crossed the shoreline with a dragging device, hoping to snag the bodies of the missing men. They spent day after flybitten day, sweating, heaving and rowing, but all that resulted was blistered hands. In the meantime, McClinton headed a party of Indians that combed the bush for miles around. They found not a trace of the missing men.

It was a disappointed police squad that finally arrived back in Vanderhoof. They had requested the Indians to watch for anything suspicious, and from Vanderhoof sent out descriptions of the missing men — and Fredericks.

The Alberta Provincial Police quickly located Fredericks at Moon Lake, Alberta. He was not approached directly, but a plain-clothes policeman circulating around the community for a day or two picked up the information that Fredericks mixed readily with settlers and talked occasionally of his trapping venture in B.C., although at times it was noted he gave conflicting answers to questions. He still had the mangy fox skin he got in exchange for the Winchester rifle, and persisted in telling that the Hudson's Bay Company had offered him $10 for the pelt. He produced a watch that he said his girl had given him, although he occasionally forgot this story and said he had picked it off a dead comrade in the war. To one man he mentioned a desire to change his name.

"A queer fellow," he was dubbed by the homesteaders, "never seems to tell the same story twice."

The B.C. Police, however, had nothing against Fredericks and all they could do was to have Alberta's police keep him under observation. Thus matters remained until three months later. Early in November Alex Prince, a Stuart Lake Indian, arrived at the Vanderhoof police station. He had discovered what seemed to be a grave at Trembleur Lake.

With snow already knee-deep it was not the best time to go looking for graves, although Prince said he had marked the site. Nevertheless, off went Constable Jennings and Prince.

Three days later they were further up the lake than on the previous search. The snow was deeper still but they finally found the markers. When Jennings removed some frozen moss he discovered fragments of underwear and a human limb. Prince watched as the policeman removed more rock and earth. A final tug on what appeared to be an old rag revealed that it enclosed a human skull.

Jennings had seen enough. Putting things back as he found them, he made a fast trip to Vanderhoof and returned with coroner W. R. Stone. Again there had been a snowfall, but with the aid of the markers they found the site. Two bodies were eventually uncovered.

At the autopsy in Vanderhoof the remains were identified as those of the missing Germans — their teeth being valuable clues. The coroner's jury decided that Westphal and Peters had been murdered "by a person or persons unknown . . . but evidence points strongly to the guilt of a man known as Karl Fredericks." The jury also commended the work of the Provincial Police, in particular Constable Jennings.

A wire to the Alberta Provincial Police quickly resulted in Fredericks being apprehended. Although formally warned, he stoutly maintained he did not know anyone called Westphal or Peters, had never been to Fort St. James, Trembleur Lake or Vanderhoof. He said he'd come to Moon Lake from the east and rode a freight.

Constable McClinton went to Alberta to bring back the suspect, and as the foothills rolled monotonously past the car windows, Fredericks persisted in talking. But this time he had a different version to the story.

He admitted that he knew the dead Germans. All three had gone into the Trembleur Lake country to sell liquor to the Indians. Peters, he said, had a bad temper and one day when they got to scuffling, Fredericks shot him in self defence. When he returned to the lakeside camp he discovered Westphal dead, apparently killed by Peters earlier in the day.

It was now five months since the double killing, and with Fredericks committed for trial, the Crown rested its case on the fact that Fredericks had concealed the bodies of his partners and failed to report their deaths. In addition, he had the watch belonging to one of the men, most of their money and had given away their cache of food. Physical evidence showed that both men had had their skulls battered in. Westphal's head was severed from his body with a sharp instrument, and wrapped in cloth and buried. Peters' skull had a bullet hole in it and was smashed into thirty-five pieces. Dirt and twigs inside his shirt were considered evidence that the dead man had been dragged to his grave. Police and medical experts were of the opinion that the two men had been murdered in their sleep.

From a layman's point of view, the affair was a double murder and a murderer's flight; from the legal profession's position it wasn't that concrete. In fact the subsequent courtroom tactics made legal history in B.C.

The tale of wilderness infamy unfolded in May 1931 when Karl Fredericks stood in the prisoner's box at the Prince George Assizes. Because the prosecutor's case was part fact, part supposition, the jury were unable to agree. A new trial was scheduled for the fall.

This time the jury reached the verdict "Guilty" and Fredericks was sentenced to death. However, he appealed the decision and won a new trial at Kamloops. This jury overturned the sentence. Fredericks walked from the courtroom a free man.

But his story didn't end. As in the fable, Death was not to be denied. Two years later, Fredericks was picked up by Game Warden W. D. Quesnel near Bridge Lake in the Cariboo, a gun under his arm. Quesnel asked him if he had a license. He hadn't. In addition, the Warden discovered that Fredericks was an alien.

A Justice of the Peace sentenced him to a $50 fine or 60 days. Fredericks decided to serve time — an unfortunate decision because when his picture and fingerprints were routinely passed on to Ottawa they were matched to those of a man charged with murder some two years before. Since Fredericks was still a German national, Ottawa passed the information to the German police. They replied that he had had six convictions before he came to Canada.

Fredericks soon found himself in the hands of Canadian Immigration, speeding across Canada to Halifax. The next ship to Germany had him aboard.

It was a homecoming with grim undertones. In Frederick's absence a little man named Adolf Hitler had taken over the German Reich and was busily exterminating all opposition, especially communists. Unfortunately, before leaving his native land Fredericks had done a little street fighting with the communists. As a consequence two S.S. men — booted, belted and armed — were waiting at the gangway when Fredericks arrived in Hamburg. They promptly introduced him to the new order by whisking him off to a concentration camp.

It was the last ever seen of the man who dodged death in British Columbia — only to keep an appointment in Hitler's version of Samara.

What Ever Happened to the Halden Family?

On a morning in early April 1921, as a chinook wind steadily drove the snow from the Cariboo benchlands, Provincial Police Sergeant George H. Greenwood of the Quesnel detachment received a letter he'd been anxiously awaiting. It was from Divisional Inspector W.L. Fernie at Kamloops. It said that a Mrs. Arthur Halden of Quesnel had previously been the widowed Mrs. Wright and prior to that, in England, had been the spinster Adah Godfrey.

The excited Greenwood read the letter to his office companion, Constable E. E. Aves. "Don't you see it? Adah Godfrey — A. G. The initials on the ring."

For a moment Aves didn't understand, then he realized the significance of Greenwood's remarks. "And what are you going to do now, Sergeant?"

"You and I," said Greenwood, "are going to arrest Mr. David Clark."

David Clark's story was too smooth. Sergeant G.H. Greenwood was convinced that he had murdered the Cariboo family. But over half a century later a mystery remains — where are the three bodies?

Remains of the Halden's farm home in 1945. It was known locally as "The Haunted House."

Hired hand David Clark, inset, kept the secret of the family's disappearance.

Later in the day, Greenwood and Aves rapped on the door of the Grandview farm 3 miles (5 km) from Quesnel. A tall, dark and well built man in his early thirties opened the door.

"You're under arrest, Clark, on a charge of theft," Greenwood said.

"Theft of what?"

"A couple of rings and a couple of brooches."

"Has Mrs. Halden come back?"

"No. She's not back."

"Then who laid the charge?"

"I did," said Greenwood, then added the time-worn formula, "You are not obliged to say anything in answer to the charge. . . ."

Thus did Provincial Police Sergeant George Hargreaves Greenwood make the Crown's opening move in an incredible story of murder, mystery and intrigue that went down in the records of the B.C. Police as "The Halden Case."

Dave Clark, so suddenly plucked from his doorstep by the Provincial Police, had come to the Cariboo from the prairie the previous year, and in July had gone to work for the Haldens. The Haldens, a quiet couple in their mid-forties, with a 14-year-old stepson, had come from southern B.C. to take up land a few miles from Quesnel. The Haldens didn't go into Quesnel very often but in late fall someone noticed that they hadn't been around at all. The hired man, Clark, explained that the three had suddenly gone to Spokane to attend the funeral of Halden's brother. A week or so after the Haldens' departure, Clark met Greenwood in Quesnel.

"I've got a bit of a problem," explained the farm hand. "In the last few months I lent the Haldens quite a bit of money and now I'm getting worried."

"Worried? Why?" the sergeant asked.

"Well, I've got a hunch that they won't be coming back. So it looks as though I'm going to get stuck for over $1,000."

"Got anything in writing?"

"Yes," said Clark, drawing a folded paper from his pocket. "I've got their promissory note. It's properly signed and everything."

"I think you'd better see a lawyer," advised Greenwood. "He'll know what to do."

On the strength of this conversation Clark contacted lawyer E. J. Avison. In the month that followed he began a court action for the return of $1,250 loaned to the Haldens, and a claim for wages of $762 owing from April to December, 1920.

Clark, under oath, claimed that, "on or shortly after October 29, 1920, the Haldens left for Spokane but notwithstanding most careful enquiries from the postmaster and all likely persons I cannot obtain any news of the whereabouts of the said defendants. I have ascertained they have left considerable obligations behind them and I believe they have left the country and do not propose to return."

He went on to declare: "I know of no way in which the summons in this action can be served and I respectfully apply for an order for service on them by deposit of summons in the Quesnel registry and by notice in the *Cariboo Observer*."

The document was sworn to before Government Agent Edgar C. Lunn on December 8, 1920. In due course County Court Judge Fred Calder granted permission to proceed with the action.

With these legalities behind him, bachelor Clark accepted an invitation to Christmas dinner at the neighboring Andersons. Thoughtfully Clark brought along Christmas stockings for the Anderson children, and something for Mrs. Anderson carefully wrapped in tissue paper. It turned out to be a pretty horseshoe brooch set with pearls. Clark had also a present for Mr. Anderson, a plain gold ring incribed "A. G. for Father, 1892."

"Here, here," protested Anderson, "I can't take a thing like this. It must be some sort of family heirloom."

"Oh, no it isn't," laughed Clark. "As a matter of fact I took it off a dead German officer in France."

That same evening, visiting other neighbors, Clark gave the wife of Captain W. E. Ekins, the local auctioneer, a handsome gold plated 29th Battalion brooch.

A week later the court instructed advertisement appeared in a New Year edition of the local *Cariboo Observer*. While there was no response from the Haldens, there were by now rumors circulating among the people who knew them. Eventually, some of this talk reached Greenwood. The account of Clark's generosity made Greenwood wonder. Then he connected it with the story of Clark's promissory note. But as Avison was handling it everything seemed proper. In the days that followed, however, Greenwood couldn't help wondering about the Haldens and their sudden departure.

He called at the post office and found there had been quite a lot of mail for the Haldens during the previous summer but that it had dwindled when a number of letters had been returned to the senders marked "Left the district. No forwarding address."

Greenwood's curiosity next took him to the telegraph office. Here a check of incoming telegrams around October 29 showed no message for the Haldens. In fact no one in the district had received a telegram from Spokane. Next call was the telephone office and there the answer was the same. There had been no long distance call summoning the Haldens to a funeral in Washington.

All very queer and most mysterious. At his office Greenwood cogitated, then came up with another idea. He would put in a report to his Divisional Officer and ask for a check on the Haldens' antecedents. All he could quote for identification was the fact that they owned Lot 6681, Group I, Cariboo district.

The report trickled down to the force's C.I.B. headquarters in Vancouver where a plainclothes man checked the land registry office. On the title deed was the rubber stamped names of Wallace and Van Roggen, a Vancouver law firm. They had handled the land deal. In reply to the detective's questions they said that they had conducted most of the Haldens' business but hadn't heard of them for some time. In fact the last letter on file was dated June 2, 1920. Through the firm, however, Mrs. Halden's sister, Thurza Hughes, was located at Parksville on Vancouver Island. She, too, was mystified by her sister's sudden absence from Quesnel.

According to Mrs. Hughes, her sister Adah had been married to a Mr. Wright in England, and on his death in 1915 came to Vancouver with her stepson, Stanley. She worked for a time in Victoria, but contracted typhoid fever and was for a time a patient in the Royal Jubilee Hospital. Later, she convalesced at the Hughes' Parksville home and in 1919 met Arthur Halden, and married him. The couple lived for a while at Wellington on Vancouver Island, then in the early spring of 1920 moved to Quesnel.

Apparently Mrs. Halden had money in England amounting to about $5,000. In May 1920 she thought of transferring these funds to a bank in Quesnel, but changed her mind when the rate of exchange took an adverse turn. Meanwhile, she bought six $50 Victory Bonds for her stepson, and these were still in the Quesnel bank.

The police next probed Arthur Halden's background. They discovered that he had no brother in Washington and official records confirmed that no one of that name had died in eastern Washington the previous fall. Furthermore, Spokane police said no one named Halden had registered at any Spokane hotel the previous October.

After Greenwood analyzed this information he checked locally and discovered that the family had stocked up with groceries just before their disappearance. If they intended to leave, why did they buy so many groceries?

The ring Clark gave away at Christmas Greenwood showed to Thurza Hughes. She promptly identified it as her sister's memorial ring on the death of her father in 1892. She also identified the pearl horseshoe brooch and produced a picture of her sister's wedding in Vancouver in 1919 showing Adah wearing it.

With this information, Sergeant Greenwood had to act quickly or the Halden's property would become Clark's by due process of law. That was why he arrested Clark on April 17, 1921, for theft. Clark stuck to the story that he had taken the gold ring from a dead German during the war, and vowed he had bought the brooch in England.

When Clark's case came before the Prince George Spring Assize in 1921, the jury could not agree. His lawyer applied for bail but since Divisional Inspector Fernie would not consent to bail under $10,000 — a sum that Clark could not raise — he stayed in jail.

According to Fernie, the prospect of Mrs. Halden's money coming from England had spurred Clark to kill the family and lay claim to the estate. But if Clark had murdered the Haldens, how, when and where had he done it?

As Clark languished in jail that summer, squads of police criss-crossed the Halden farm and neighboring countryside. They employed scores of skilled Indian trackers in an attempt to pick up any fragments of information that might be the key to unlocking the Cariboo mystery.

The farmhouse was searched from roof to basement. Walls were tapped, floors torn up and the earth basement floor excavated and sifted. Nearby ditches and sloughs were probed and days spent dragging nearby Dragon Lake. Wherever there was the appearance of a slash fire, the soil was sifted to a considerable depth. Wells were pumped and back eddies in the Quesnel River explored. After weeks of searching, however, the tired and frustrated Provincial Police had to admit the Halden family had vanished.

Then in November Clark was tried for a second time, again at Prince George. On this occasion, however, the verdict was "guilty." The judge sentenced Clark to two years.

While the smug-faced Clark spent his days in the turreted penitentiary on the banks of the Fraser at New Westminster, the police continued their search for the Haldens. A $1,000 reward was offered but failed to prompt any response. Another angle considered by the police was that if Clark had loaned the Haldens $1,250, he may have had a bank account. Asked about it in the penitentiary, Clark with a smile told the police that he didn't believe in banks. He always kept his money in a belt around his waist.

"You carried $1,250 around with you?" suggested the investigator.

"Sure," said Clark.

While searching the Halden farmhouse the police couldn't help noting one significant fact. There wasn't a letter or a document in the place bearing the Halden signatures, and not a single photograph of the couple. All had been destroyed, the twisted and melted picture frames were found in the ashes of a bedroom heater.

Greenwood, however, made an interesting discovery. A blotter, held to a mirror, showed that someone had been practicing Halden's signature. Fortunately, at the law firm of Wallace & Van Roggen there were still the authentic Halden signatures. These were checked with the signatures on Clark's promissory note, which a handwriting expert promptly branded as a forgery. So did Thurza Hughes, accustomed to seeing her sister's signature.

In the fall of 1923 the main gate of the penitentiary at New Westminster swung open to release Clark. His freedom was brief. Waiting was a Provincial Police Sergeant with a warrant, charging him with forgery. That December before Mr. Justice Aulay Morrison and a New Westminster jury, David Arthur Clark stood, a half-quizzical smile on his face, and pleaded "not guilty."

From then on Crown Counsel George Cassidy drew from witnesses one of the strangest stories aired in a British Columbia courtroom. It recounted those toilsome weeks around the Grandview farm where the police delved and probed for a trace of three people who, the Crown felt sure, had been murdered.

Perhaps the ghosts of the Haldens were hovering in the courtroom, especially when Clark's lawyer asked Mrs. Hughes why she referred to her sister as the "late" Mrs. Halden. "You have no proof that she is dead," he suggested.

"Oh, she's dead all right," was Mrs. Hughes quiet reply.

The motive for the forgery was reviewed, including Clark's brazen attempt through the Quesnel court action to take over the estate of this missing couple.

"His clumsy efforts to delude the law were unavailing," was the way Judge Morrison summarized to the jury.

On Friday, December 13, the jury retired. They returned in an hour with the verdict that David Arthur Clark was guilty.

"Have you anything to say before I pass sentence?" asked Judge Morrison. The entire court waited, expecting Clark to make some sort of admission.

With his customary smile, Clark bowed to the bench, "Your Lordship." Then, as an afterthought, he turned to the packed courtroom and added, "and ladies and gentlemen."

"You are not here to make a speech," said the Judge, as he cut him off. "The law entitles me to give you a maximum sentence of fourteen years imprisonment. However, I'm not in agreement with long sentences, and I'm going to give you ten years."

It is now well over half a century since the Haldens vanished from their Quesnel homestead. In those decades not a trace of them has been found.

The Men Who Were Murdered by Mistake

It was unfortunate that Jim Miller so closely resembled the Nanaimo hangman. But did justice prevail when his murderer was set free?

On the morning of February 14, 1886, George A. Lilley rode up to Jim Miller's cabin which fronted the beach of Osborne Bay on the southeast coast of Vancouver Island between Victoria and Nanaimo. In the neighborly fashion of the day, Lilley was bringing Miller his mail. As he dismounted he noticed an extra horse in the lean-to that functioned as a stable. Jim Miller and Bill Dring, the only settlers fronting the bay, had two things in common. Both were bachelors and both loved a drink.

"Another bright night," mused Lilley, thinking of their well-known get-togethers. As he pushed open the front door he wasn't surprised to find Dring lying over the table and Miller flat on his back on the floor.

"And a good morning to both of you," was Lilley's hearty greeting as he slapped the mail on the table. He studied the recumbent Miller with

amusement. "Come on, Jim, get up," he urged, nudging Miller with his foot.

As his eyes adjusted to the cabin's gloom, Lilley's cheerfulness changed to shock when he realized that Miller had taken his last drink. His throat had been cut from ear to ear!

Lilley turned in horror to Dring, only to see that his throat also was slit. He backed quickly out of the cabin and in seconds was galloping toward the nearest settlement, Chemainus, to break the news to B.C. Provincial Police Constable Daniel W. Mainguy.

Mainguy, with coroner W. W. Walkem, saddled up and was soon on the scene. Their investigation disclosed that Dring and Miller, as usual had been drinking the night before, and were apparently starting their evening meal when death overtook them. On the table were two half empty plates of soup, a piece of bread beside each plate, and a coal-oil lamp, empty of oil, the wick charred and hard.

Miller, they deduced, had stood and turned to face the door when he got a charge of buckshot in the stomach. He had staggered and fallen on his back near the fireplace. Dring had apparently been shot through the

The lonely foreshore cabin where Miller and Dring were murdered. Although Superintendent H. B. Roycraft, opposite, solved the mystery, the killer went free.

head while sitting at the table. As he didn't die immediately, his assailant had cut his throat.

Perhaps by this time Miller had tried to rise and had received a rifle ball in the chest. He was then stabbed through the heart and his throat was cut, almost certainly after death, Walkem felt.

The investigators believed that two or more persons had carried out the diabolical attack since two weapons had been used, and there was no sign of a struggle. An old Kentucky rifle slung by a cord over the fireplace had not been handled or fired recently. Robbery did not appear to be the motive for under Miller's bed they discovered a tin box containing about $100.

Searching outside the building, Mainguy found tracks leading to the beach. Here, in the mud, he was able to discern fresh footprints, evidence of a fire, and signs that a canoe had been pulled up and launched again. Mingling with the boot prints were tracks made by bare feet, possibly by a youngster or a woman.

Mainguy poured hot tallow into the footprints to preserve them, then returned to the cabin to continue his investigation. He discovered a bullet hole in one of the windows and by aligning its direction had the luck to find a bullet embedded in a snake fence. It was a cast bullet from a rough mould that might have belonged to an Indian.

This discovery, added to the manner of the killing, the tracks on the beach, and the evidence of a canoe, indicated that the killers could have been Indians. But if robbery wasn't the motive, it must have been revenge. For what? George Lilley, who lived ten minutes away on the trail, was positive the two bachelors hadn't an enemy in the country.

Constable Mainguy checked the settler's background but found nothing unusual. James Miller was a Scot, just over 60, who had seen the 1849 California gold rush when he was 25. Ten years later he joined the stampede to British Columbia's Fraser River gold rush. He was the first man to take up a pre-emption at Osborne Bay in 1866, and in the next twenty years acquired additional property that added up to 136 acres (55 ha).

Adjoining his land was the larger tract of the only other waterfront settler, William Henry Dring. Dring had come from northern Ireland. He was a big man, taller than average and at the time of his death aged 46, though hard drinking made him look older.

When news of the crime was received at Police Headquarters in Victoria, some 50 miles (80 km) down the coast, Superintendent H. B. Roycraft spurred his men up and down the 300-mile (480-km) east coast of Vancouver Island to immediate action. However, as weeks developed into months, no clue turned up.

Then eighteen months later in July 1887, a report was received from Alert Bay detachment at the north end of the Island. A little schooner called *Seabird* was overdue and was thought to have been attacked by Indians. By rare coincidence, Roycraft was in the locality and took personal charge of the investigation. He eventually found the *Seabird* on a creek that runs into Blenkinsop Bay, just east of Port Neville in Johnstone Strait. Evidently the schooner had been towed up the creek and set on fire to cover traces of the murder of its captain, Harry Moore, and his two-man crew.

Nanaimo in the 1880s. The bastion at upper left near the center of the photo has been preserved and is today a museum.

Roycraft learned that Moore, a one-armed man, always had the left sleeve removed from his coats and shirts. When he eventually found an Indian with one of Moore's armless shirts he was able to solve the triple murder on the *Seabird* and arrest the killer, a Salmon River Indian named Macmoose from nearby Kelsey Bay on Vancouver Island.

In the course of the *Seabird* investigation, Roycraft picked up scraps of a strange story involving the killing of two white men the previous year near Chemainus, an obvious reference to Miller and Dring.

Roycraft's principal informant was an Indian woman named Sally At-loo-mult who said she could identify the man who did the killing. With Sally aboard a government steamer, Roycraft visited the farming settlement at Comox, south of Alert Bay, and on August 8 had a suspect in custody. He was Quomlet, a Salmon River Indian. Quomlet was a little surprised to see Sally and as he passed her whispered, "Keep your mouth shut and I'll give you a big canoe."

The whispered warning, however, did not pass unheard by Roycraft.

According to Sally's story, Quomlet's accomplice in the murder of Miller and Dring was another Salmon River man, Johnny Kla-quot-sie. But Quomlet, questioned about Johnny's whereabouts, merely said Johnny was beyond the law's clutches. He had been frozen to death in his canoe the previous winter.

As Roycraft probed into the Miller-Dring killing, he uncovered one of the most dramatic stories in B.C.'s crime annals.

As Sally related it, there had been a big Indian gathering at Salmon River in November 1885, during which a fight developed and an Indian called Talaguna killed a fellow tribesman, Quom-kack-elak-is. Among eye-witnesses to the deed was Quomlet. He had more than passing interest in the killing for Talaguna, the man who wielded the knife, was his younger brother; the murdered man was his father-in-law; and Sally was Talaguna's daughter.

Talaguna was convicted of the murder at Nanaimo in December 1885, and it was largely Quomlet's evidence as Crown witness that put the rope around his brother's neck. But while it was an action that satisfied Quomlet's wife, who mourned her murdered father, it turned Sally against him. She felt that Quomlet had caused the death of her father.

The night after Talaguna's execution at Nanaimo, Quomlet and the two women occupied a cabin on the nearby foreshore at Departure Bay. That night, around the fire built on the cabin's earth floor, Quomlet was torn by conflicting emotions. Near him in one corner Sally mourned her father, blaming Quomlet for giving evidence that had sent him to his death. Quomlet thought of his younger brother being hanged and guilt overwhelmed him. He must find a way to make peace with Sally, avenge his brother's death and restore his own honor.

The man who had acted as public executioner that morning was a Nanaimo teamster named Dick. A tough and calloused frontiersman from Missouri, he believed in the Western adage that "the only good Indian is a dead Indian." Dick hadn't minded the role of hangman, in fact he rather relished it. Although it was customary for the executioner to be hooded, Dick scorned the idea of hiding his identity and wore no mask.

He also had a pre-emption not far from Miller's at Osborne Bay. Here, in pauses between work, he visited Miller, and people seeing them together were struck by their resemblance to each other. They had many times been taken for brothers. For Miller, this resemblance was to be tragic.

After brooding on his problem for several days, Quomlet came to a conclusion — he would have to kill the hangman. In this way he would avenge his brother's death on the gallows, and Sally would respect him. In his mind, Quomlet was sure that Miller was the hangman. He had to die.

Quomlet bought a hunting knife from a Nanaimo trader, and a week after the hanging of Talaguna, left Departure Bay in his canoe with Johnny Kla-quot-sie and Sally. With them were two bottles of whisky, a rifle, shotgun and the knife. The shotgun was an old Hudson's Bay muzzle-loading musket charged with odd scraps of metal. The rifle was a Winchester with hand-loaded cartridges.

After reconnoitering Osborne Bay, they landed on the beach near Miller's cabin. According to Sally, they huddled, unobserved, round a small beach fire until darkness descended. Then Quomlet climbed the bank carrying the rifle, followed by Johnny with the shotgun. Sally stayed behind. Shortly after, she heard two shots, followed quickly by two more.

Minutes later Quomlet and Johnny returned with a sack of flour. Quomlet went back to get a clock from the cabin, then the trio paddled north to Nanaimo. At Sharp's Point they hid the clock and the flour and finished the whisky, throwing away the empty bottle.

It was March 1888 — two years after the double killing at Osborne Bay — when this story unfolded. On Roycraft's instruction, Constable J.

94

M. Langley took Sally to Nanaimo. Starting from Departure Bay, they retraced the route the killers had taken. Langley found evidence of the fire at Sharp's Point, and retrieved the weathered sack of flour and Miller's clock, as well as the empty whisky bottle.

Meanwhile, as the Nanaimo Spring Assize drew near it was obvious that Quomlet would not be able to face a judge and jury. He was in the last stages of tuberculosis and, in fact, died in the Nanaimo Jail on July 9.

Although Johnny Kla-quot-sie was reported to be dead, there were doubts in Roycraft's mind. He continued to search for him and two weeks after Quomlet's death found Johnny in an upcoast hide-out. A week later he was locked up in Victoria's Bastion Square Jail, charged with the murder of Miller.

The police had done a lot of good work in unravelling the mysterious double murder; work that in two years took many man-hours. Now, as the case was about to be concluded, Roycraft made an unusual compromise, promising Johnny immunity if he told the truth. Johnny told the truth — and saved his neck.

At the preliminary hearing, Victoria's Stipendiary Magistrate Edwin Brown held Johnny's admission inadmissible as evidence. He refused to commit him to trial.

"But the corroborative evidence of Sally?" interjected Roycraft.

"I'm afraid she isn't a credible witness," was the Magistrate's reply, referring to evidence from the Constable who had searched Quomlet's cabin after the murders. Sally had told him that the two men present, Quomlet and Kla-quot-sie, had not left the cabin on the weekend of the murders.

"She has told two stories," said the Magistrate. Then he quoted the well-established formula in Canadian law: "Confessions and admissions of accused persons obtained by promise of immunity are inadmissible as evidence." He had no alternative but to discharge the accused.

Thus it was that Kla-quot-sie found himself in August a free man outside Victoria's grim Bastion Square Jail. Undoubtedly guilty, he escaped because of a legal technicality. He wasn't the first, nor was he the last. But one question remains — did the murdered men receive justice?

A Policeman Dies

**Constable Isaac Decker had a remarkable memory — and a
devotion to duty that ended his life.**

On an afternoon in late June 1887, a lone horseman galloped his sweat-
streaked bay mount through the verdant bottomland of the lower Similka-
meen Valley in southern B.C. The impatient rider was a tall lean cowpuncher named Frank Spencer with one finger missing. The horse he was riding
was stolen, so was the saddle and bridle, and the .44 Winchester in the scab-
bard alongside his leg.

Spencer was fleeing because he had shot and killed a fellow cowboy
near Kamloops about a week before over a bottle of rye. But that wasn't
his first lawless act. Orphaned in Tennessee, Spencer was already wild when
he hit Texas at 16. From there he brawled and gunfought until at 20 he
was in Dodge City. Here, history reminds us, Marshall "Mysterious Dave"
Mathers killed seven men in one night, and twenty-five men were killed
and fifty wounded in one bullet-splattered year.

The youthful Spencer was jailed there a couple of times before moving on to Tombstone, Arizona, where he teamed up with the infamous Clan-
ton gang raiding Mexican cattle ranches. But in 1881 the lawless element
were decimated when the Earp brothers, along with "Doc" Holliday, took
on the Clantons at the OK corral; Jesse James was shot; and Billy the Kid
eliminated at White Oaks, New Mexico.

Frank Spencer got the message. In order to stay above ground he made
for southeastern Arizona, then drifted to Colorado and worked his way

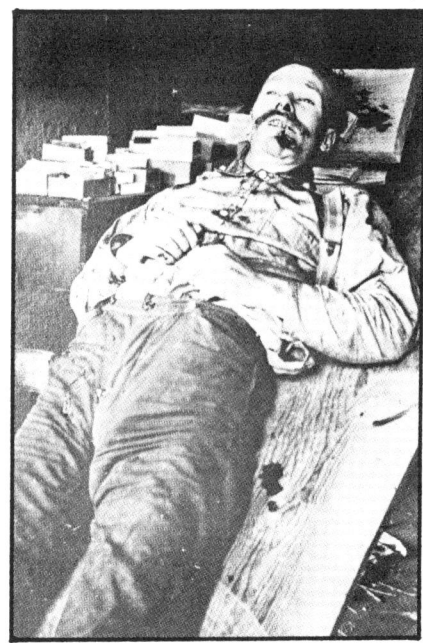

**Train robber Dave Haney who was
shot dead by Constable Decker.**

**Despite the $4,000 reward offered
for William Haney, opposite page,
he was never seen again.**

96

$4,000.00 REWARD $4,000.00

The Government of the Province of British Columbia hereby offers a reward of TWO THOUSAND FIVE HUNDRED DOLLARS for the arrest and conviction of WILLIAM HANEY, who, on the night of the 28th day of June, 1909, near Ashcroft in the said Province, shot and killed one Isaac Decker, a Special Constable.

WILLIAM HANEY
PHOTOGRAPH TAKEN IN 1896

WILLIAM HANEY
LATEST PHOTOGRAPH OBTAINABLE

In addition to the reward of Two Thousand Five Hundred Dollars, offered by the Government of British Columbia,

The Canadian Pacific Railway Co. offers a further reward of One Thousand Five Hundred Dollars

making a total reward of Four Thousand Dollars, payable on the terms above mentioned.

Description of WILLIAM HANEY American

AGE—About thirty-eight years.

HEIGHT—Five feet eight inches.

WEIGHT—About 180 pounds.

BUILD—Well built and muscular. Has slightly swinging, lazy walk, from side to side like a sailor; drags feet.

COMPLEXION—Medium.

HAIR—Mixed with grey. Slightly bald on crown, has "cowlick" and usually combs hair back. Forehead high at sides.

EYES—Blue, almost grey.

FACE—Broad, flat features. Nose normal between eyes, but grows quite large at end—end of nose red and fleshy. Large nostrils. **Large ears. TWO MOLES ON RIGHT CHEEK.**

HANDS—Thick, fat hands; hair on hands quite thick and coarse.

MARKS—Large mole on top of right shoulder. Large vaccination mark on right upper arm. One small scar back of head.

Wire any information to the undersigned.

By Order,

F. S. HUSSEY,
Superintendent, Provincial Police.

Provincial Police Department,
Victoria, B. C.
3rd August, 1909.

WINTER EDITION

north to Montana. He was rustling horses there when members of the Stock Growers' Association decided to take the law into their own hands. Under the leadership of "Strangler" Stuart, the Association hoisted a lot of characters up the nearest tree. By the neck, that is. All had the misfortune to have someone else's brand on their stock.

It was time for Spencer to move again. This time he crossed the Canadian line into the region that became Alberta. Finally, in 1886, he rode the first Canadian Pacific Railway train as far as Kamloops. Here, a year later, he shot and killed Pete Foster in the corral of Campbell's Ranch. Promptly he left on one of Campbell's horses, pursued by Provincial Police Constable Walter H. Smith and two Indian trackers. The lawman pursued him clear to the United States border but, without the aid of telephone or telegraph, there was little chance of interception.

Three years later Spencer's luck was shattered by a B.C. Provincial Policeman with an uncanny memory. At the time Spencer was working for a Pendleton, Oregon, horsebreeder who by odd chance was readying some horses to ship to New Westminster, B.C.

Although Spencer, in occasional bunkhouse confidences, had hinted that he once had some trouble with the law in Canada, he now decided that was all in the past and agreed to travel north with the horses. One of his fellow horse wranglers did remark that he might be taking a bit of a chance. As he succinctly put it: "Up there in Canada, Frank, the law only gives you one shake of the dice." The words proved to be deadly prophetic.

On his second day in New Westminster, Spencer strolled into a bar on Columbia Street. He had just ordered a drink when a stranger touched him on the arm. The stranger identified himself as Provincial Constable Isaac Decker, and informed Spencer that he was under arrest for the murder of Pete Foster at Kamloops some three years before.

If Spencer was flabbergasted he had a right to be. He had never been in custody in B.C. and perhaps only a dozen people around Kamloops would have recognized him. Yet here was this Provincial Policeman from Ashcroft who'd never seen Spencer before picking him up by the description on a three-year-old circular. No photo, just a written description of a murderer with a missing finger.

In typically expeditious style of the day, within a month Spencer was tried at Kamloops Spring Assize. On the bench was Mr. Justice G. A. Walkem wearing, probably to the prisoner's wonderment, a wig. The jury said "guilty," and forty days later Frank Spencer was hanged at the Kamloops jail. The tough cowboy from Dodge City and points south had one final but rather curious wish. He didn't want to die with his boots on. So he wore carpet slippers to the scaffold and when he was buried in the jail yard.

Constable Decker, the policeman with the uncanny memory for circulars, served a few more years in the B.C. Provincial Police. Then he took up a ranch near Spences Bridge, 25 miles (40 km) from Ashcroft.

In June 1909, two decades after the Spencer trial, Decker received a telegram from the District Chief of Provincial Police at Ashcroft, Joe Burr — great uncle of Raymond Burr who one day would portray on TV the super-efficient attorney Perry Mason and the wheelchair sleuth Ironside.

The telegram was short. Because of an emergency, could Decker fill in for a few days as a Special Constable?

A Canadian Pacific Railway train had just been held up near Kamloops in the same manner and place where Bill Miner had held up a train three years before. (See Heritage House book, *Bill Miner — STAGECOACH & TRAIN ROBBER*.)

Three men were said to be involved and police thought there was the chance they might come down the Thompson River by boat. Decker promptly responded and Burr posted him on the river bank just outside Ashcroft.

A day later, around dusk, a skiff appeared with two men in it. When Decker spotted them, he pumped the lever action of his Winchester, then yelled to the boatmen to come ashore.

With some difficulty the inexperienced oarsmen manoeuvered the boat to the shore and hauled it up the bank. As they walked towards him, Decker noticed one of them carrying a coat over his arm — a coat that Decker quickly realized screened a revolver. Decker fired from the hip, the .44 slug catching the coat-carrying man on the point of his chin. With spilt-second reaction his partner returned the fire. Decker dropped, a bullet through his heart.

Sole witness to this deadly gunplay was an Indian woman leaning over the bridge nearby. She saw the survivor of the shoot-out stoop and take something from his dead companion's pocket. Then with a sort of loping trot, he disappeared into a clump of willows.

A mounted posse, Indian trackers and bloodhounds were soon combing the region. But though the search continued for weeks, the fugitive had simply vanished.

There was one lead. A cheap suitcase found in the bandit's skiff yielded a snapshot of an unnamed group. Copies of the photo were sent to police on the U.S. Pacific Coast. It was finally linked to a house in Long Beach, California, where investigators discovered the parents of the train-robbing duo. They identified the dead man as Dave Haney; the fugitive was his older brother, Bill.

He was never caught. Even though the search lasted ten years he never appeared in any North American prison or police station — or anywhere else.

The B.C. government and the CPR posted rewards totalling $4,000 for his capture. In addition, the CPR set aside $2,500 to help educate Isaac Decker's son, Archie, who was 12 when his father died in the line of duty.

The Railway company intended to offer Archie a job when he graduated from school. However, in 1914 World War One intervened. A year later young Archie joined the army and was posted to France with the 1st Pioneer Battalion in March 1916. Brief, however, was his share of life. He was killed in action three months later. Father and son deserve a memorial for service to their country.

The Unfortunate Jerry Hill and Free Enterprise

In 1885 Jerry Hill rode innocently into what is today Revelstoke — his two packhorses laden with liquor, a provincial license to sell it. The consequence was truly astonishing.

"The Kootenays," pioneer newspaper editor Bob Lowery once remarked, "are short of frills, boiled shirts, parsons, lawyers and prohibition orators, but plentifully supplied with mule skinners, packers, trail blazers and remittance men."

This summary by a newspaperman who became a legend is a good introduction to the thousands of free-swinging, hard-drinking characters who built the Canadian Pacific Railway in the early 1880s and in whose polyglot wake shanty towns like Summit City in Rogers Pass and Farwell on the Columbia River sprang into prominence. Today Farwell — now Revelstoke

An 1889 photo of Revelstoke showing the Columbia Hotel and east end of Lower Town — or Farwell as it was first called.

— lives only in historic photographs and newspaper clippings but in its brief fling at life became somewhat famous — or infamous. It was the site of a confrontation between B.C. Provincial Police, the North-West Mounted Police (today the RCMP) and a force known as "Dominion Constables." Some say the Farwell affair stemmed from a clash between Federal and Provincial liquor laws. Maybe so. At the time in the Northwest Territories (the prairies) there was theoretical prohibition, whereas B.C.'s statute law allowed people to drink anything, anywhere, anytime, so long as they paid for it.

Licensees, at least in the Kootenays, had to provide accommodation for a minimum of six guests. Along the line of construction camps this requirement was easily met by putting six cots at the end of the barroom and screening them with a sheet. While not providing much privacy, the arrangement did comply with the law. The restaurant was usually the free lunch counter, and while the proprietor's wife sat up half the night dealing stud poker (appropriating 10 per cent from every pot), her husband tended the bar. This happy situation could go on night and day, seven days a week.

The Provincial Police, very few and very scattered, were strung from the Rockies to the Coast and only interceded in a fight when some spoilsport drew a gun or a knife, or was caught in an act of thievery, considered an exceedingly low crime.

With crisp economy of words Interior papers reported (in 1885) such doings as: "Frank Hutchins came to town . . . was indulging too freely on Sunday; Monday morning his body was found near the north side of Main Street. He is believed to have fallen and broken his neck. Buried at government expense."

At Fort Steele: "A few days ago Joe, a half-breed packer for R. L. Galbraith, stabbed his brother-in-law on the Kootenay River. While Mr. Rykert was viewing the body the murderer went out and hanged himself."

Near Eagle Pass: "William Leonard quit work on the 24th, and was found two weeks later three-quarters of a mile from the river, a bullet in the back of his head. Been dragged off the road and dumped in the bush. He was a whisky peddler."

At Black Canyon on the CPR line Bill Ableshire killed a man called Carey in a gladiatorial shovel versus knife fight, and when a Shuswap ferryman picked a fight with a passenger, shotgun versus revolver, "Provincial Constable Charles Todd reached out his hand for the revolver saying, 'I'll take the pistol, you take a sleep,' and the danger was over."

This was the year that Baird, a lone United States traveller, was found dead at Kicking Horse Pass near Golden, and his murderer, "Bulldog" Kelly, was pursued clear to Minneapolis. On the North Thompson River, John Everson killed Louis Wallshed and vanished . . . to Victoria. There, two months later, he was picked up as he window shopped in Trounce Alley.

Another newspaper account related how Provincial Constable Jack Kirkup arrived in Kamloops with William Brown "accused of murdering Mary Purcell in the Montana Saloon" — a mere tent in the mountains — and brought along with him for good measure "The Big Kid" who got three years for theft, and "Shoo Fly," locked up for eighteen months for drawing a gun on a constable.

102

These were a few of the social highlights of 1885 when on an afternoon in mid July Irish-born Jerry Hill innocently rode into Farwell with eight cases of whisky on two pack-horses and an unshaken belief in the free enterprise system. The uproar he caused was truly astonishing, especially since a provincial liquor license in his pocket proved that he was no bootlegger.

Jerry Hill was going into business where the railroaders were thickest, although only construction trains were running. He was also triggering a bureaucratic nightmare. As an aid to sobriety the Dominion government had established some small detachments of North-West Mounted Police between Donald and Farwell. Unfortunately, that April Louis Riel's rebellion had caused the Mounties' commanding officer, the efficient Sam Steele, to be hurriedly called east. In his place had come George Hope Johnston, gazetted at Ottawa in May as a "Commissioner of Police for British Columbia" and a justice of the peace. One immediate problem was that Ottawa had no business — or right — to appoint a B.C. "Commissioner of Police." Nevertheless, Johnston immediately strengthened Farwell's four-man NWMP detachment with additional "Dominion Constables."

Although Ottawa had proclaimed a ban on liquor ten miles each side of construction, the Mounties quickly found the edict as hard to enforce as it was on the prairies. However, Johnston enthusiastically settled to the task of eradicating the demon rum — or anything else alcoholic. As a consequence, one afternoon Jerry Hill was summarily relieved of his cargo.

A little puzzled — and displaying his B.C. liquor license — he went over to see the magistrate, Malcolm Sproat. Assisting Sproat were Provincial Constables Jack Kirkup, John "Paddy" Miles and Arthur Hubbard. Ontario-born Kirkup, diplomatic and muscular, was to become something of a legend in B.C.'s law enforcement story, one of his accomplishments keeping the peace in the mining community of Rossland, unaided. Since he weighed 300 pounds (136 kilograms), it wasn't surprising.

Of him, B.C. historian Elsie G. Turnbull wrote: "Constable Kirkup treated the unruly element with a heavy hand. His method of control consisted of 'pounding, instead of impounding, offenders'. "

Kirkup's answer to drunkeness was to lock up the drunk then go after the saloon keeper. "Many a bartender learned to keep his difficult customers out of sight until they were normal again," Turnbull noted. "Kirkup sometimes encouraged 'tanked' miners to fight, believing a little exercise would help work the whisky out of their pores. If men were long on talk and short on performance it wasn't unknown for Kirkup to bump heads together until he got them mad and then set them down to finish it."

Then there is the story of a boxing match in Rossland staged by two shysters from Spokane. Unfortunately for them, Kirkup was chosen to referee. Knowing that they had been faking their bouts, he brought them together in the ring. "Boys," he said quietly, "I don't want to see any flim flam here. I want to see a spirited exhibition. And to ensure that it is, the loser's going to get three months in jail."

With strong-willed Provincial policemen such as Kirkup backing Magistrate Sproat who undoubtedly resented the Federal intrusion into Pro-

Those involved in the Farwell fiasco included Provincial Policeman Jack Kirkup, at left; Magistrate M. Sproat, top right; and Colonel J. F. Macleod, ex-Commissioner of the NWMP.
Opposite page: Colonel Sam Steele and his NWMP at Donald in 1885.

vincial domain, a judicial conflagration quickly erupted over Jerry Hill and his attempt to embrace free enterprise. The precise facts are hard to unravel, but a man called Ruddick was involved. He was probably one of Johnston's Dominion Constables, and for whom, on account of Jerry Hill's rightful complaint that Ruddick had lifted his booze, B.C. Police Constables Miles and Hubbard had a warrant.

The Provincials found Ruddick, but in a rapid change of events their prisoner was wrested from them and they were imprisoned in the Mounted Police barracks. Miles, in some ingenious fashion, escaped to report the story to Sproat. Hubbard, meanwhile, was summarily sentenced to fourteen days by Johnston — not a friendly way to treat a policeman who was simply carrying out his orders.

That a Mounted Police Sergeant was arrested by Kirkup late that night probably had little bearing on the matter. The Sergeant had imbibed a little too freely in one of the local gin mills and, making his way home, fell through the window of a Chinese laundry. Though embarrassing, it was something that could have happened to anyone. Equally embarrassing to the Federals was that next morning a Mounted Police Corporal came to explain to the Provincials that the Sergeant was needed as a witness in a case.

"Have him back here in an hour," was Kirkup's edict, and apparently the gentlemanly agreement was adhered to.

The jailing of Hubbard, however, was more serious, especially as the constabulary byplay had become common knowledge, and the town was in a bit of an uproar. So much so that Johnston and his Dominion police force were virtually besieged.

Kirkup suggested swearing in about twenty specials and storming the Federal bastille, but Sproat had a more legal approach. He issued warrants for the arrest of Johnston and his two chief assistants, Rhodes and Fane. Kirkup made the arrests, unaided. He was all policeman.

One comical aspect in the now ridiculous affair was when Sproat sent a man called Garden, with a white flag of truce, to get some of Johnston's personal belongings. The lockup door was opened a crack and a gun stuck in Garden's face.

"Garden, being an old soldier," runs the official report, ". . . merely laughed."

Sproat reported the situation to the Attorney-General in Victoria, intimating that everything was under control and no assistance was needed, although he did say "he (Johnston) threatened to arrest myself and every officer connected with the province . . . he and his men marched into the chief streets of town like cowboys on a raid."

Of the "siege" he noted: "These policemen seem frightened out of their wits by their situation before the law and the prompt incarceration of their ringleader."

When news of the constabulary crisis reached Ottawa, the reaction was the prompt appearance of Colonel J. F. Macleod, an ex-Commissioner of the North-West Mounted Police. Macleod, a level-headed man, seems to have soon realized that the representatives of the Dominion government were far from capable.

The problem the two men had to resolve, Sproat noted in formal but somewhat difficult to understand words, was that there ". . . was no question of constitutionality of acts and no question as to the license involved in the offence which was simply a flagrant obstruction of the administration of provincial justice in its temperate exercise."

In plain words, the now baffled Jerry Hill and his valid liquor license was of secondary importance; obstruction of the Provincial Police was the point at issue.

Macleod apparently felt the same way. Sproat told Victoria: ". . . neither the officer commanding the North-West Mounted Police here nor anybody else competent to judge attempts to defend the dominion police."

Johnston, meantime, sitting in his provincial cell, must have wondered how he got into such a muddle so quickly.

Sproat asked Colonel Macleod to sit on the case with him for, as he put it, sitting alone he could only commit the accused to the next Kamloops Assize. Two magistrates, however, could deal with the accused immediately. As a consequence, on the morning of August 30, 1885, Sproat and Macleod took their places on the bench to view a motley group which included four uniformed Mounted Policemen and a very downcast Johnston. He pleaded "Not guilty," then changed his mind and said, "Guilty."

He was charged with obstructing Provincial Constables John Miles and Arthur Hubbard and "aiding and abetting the release of James Ruddick."

Constable Kirkup addressed the court with the suggestion that the charges be reduced to common assault.

"Do you speak on behalf of the two Constables aggrieved?" asked Magistrate Sproat.

"I do," said Kirkup. "They don't wish for a vindictive penalty, but only ask that their position be made clear."

With this request granted, Magistrate Sproat then spoke of the seriousness of the offence, and the fact that it was punishable by six months hard labor and, if need be, a $100 fine — over four months' pay for a Mountie. "The position I make clear in a few words," he concluded. "A notion prevails that in these cases there is a question between the Dominion and the Province. This is not so. It is the law of Canada that is concerned, the law that I chiefly administer in this court and as a token of the unity and diversity of our Canadian institutions, I am glad that, in these cases today, to have associated with me a distinguished judge from a sister territory on the other side of the mountains."

On this gracious and amiable note, "Commissioner of Police" Johnston, guilty of three charges of assault, was fined $10 on each count, plus $9.75 costs.

Colonel Macleod then left the bench, and Magistrate Sproat addressed himself to the four Mounties who had all pleaded guilty: "I am remitting you all to your officers for trial."

There was a last word. It came from Kirkup who reminded the court that Johnston's Dominion Constables had all fled town, including the five who put Constable Paddy Miles in a cell. "Prepare warrants for their arrest," ordered Sproat.

"Thus," the Kamloops paper later noted, ". . . ended a somewhat startling action on the part of the magistrate but the authority of his court had been memorably and completely vindicated."

Johnston slipped quietly away and in due course the Mounties welcomed back the much more capable Sam Steele.

While no grudges apparently surfaced over the affair, neither did Jerry Hill's liquor. In some suspicious manner the constabulary lost it in the shuffle! The sequel, however, was almost as funny as the siege of Farwell.

A Victoria citizen who put up the money for the liquor took legal action against Jerry Hill who must by now have had his faith in free enterprise somewhat shattered. That fall Provincial Constable George Wright at Kamloops found a writ of capias in his mail. More familiar with cattle brands than capias, Wright consulted Government Agent Tunstall who said, "It's an authority to hold Jerry until the debt's satisfied. You'll have to lock him up."

To the free and easy Constable Wright this action seemed hardly in keeping with the code of the West. He compromised. Jerry was to turn up at the provincial jail every night to be locked up, but could spend his days as he pleased. A time limit of three months was agreed upon.

Thus by day Jerry propped up the bar of Ned Cannell's Saloon, and each night banged on the jail door for entry.

Came spring, and as the first chinook wafted the snow from the benchlands, one night a note was found on Jerry's cell bunk. It said simply that now that it was spring it was time for him to go, and thanks very much for the kind treatment.

Wright scratched his head and thought of the Victoria creditor. Surely there must be some sort of legal termination to this quaint deal. He consulted Tunstall again.

"Send the sheriff at Victoria a bill for three months' board and lodging," said Tunstall, with a grin, "and I'll bet you never hear another word." They never did!

A few months later the chime whistle of the first transcontinental train was heard through the mountain passes of the Rockies, by which time the Supreme Court of Canada had ruled that British Columbia controlled its own liquor laws. In a way, this ruling makes Jerry Hill the patron saint of B.C.'s Liquor Control Board. But Jerry, like everyone else involved, was probably far more interested in forgetting his venture into private enterprise than being a patron saint.

The Cariboo's Stagecoach Bandits

**The stagecoach robber didn't know that each creek stamps its
identification on the gold it yields. Chief Constable Fred Hussey
did know — and so did the Cariboo jury.**

For some fifty years from the early 1860s to World War One, the Cariboo
Wagon Road from Yale to Barkerville 400 miles (645 km) to the northward
was the main street of miners, cattlemen, settlers and all others who ventured into the Cariboo. Today a paved highway, in its long history it has
seen more types of transportation than probably any other road in North
America.

At first men walked over the route, their possessions on their back.
One of them, Billy Ballou, became the first mailman, carrying letters the
400 miles (645 km) to Barkerville for $1 each. Other means of transporta-

tion were camels, steam traction engines, packhorses, dog sleds, and huge wagons drawn by horses, mules and oxen. Here, too, were the yellow and red stagecoaches of the B.C. Express Company, the famous "B.X." that operated on a regular schedule, whatever the weather. In the early 1860s stagecoach service began from Yale and continued until construction of the Canadian Pacific Railway in the early 1880s destroyed the Cariboo Wagon Road through the Fraser Canyon. Then service began at a new community called Ashcroft, and continued for another thirty years until completion of the Pacific Great Eastern Railway ended the stagecoach era.

During the decades of service the B.X. built an outstanding reputation for reliability and service. In 1866 the New Westminster paper, the *British Columbian*, commented:

". . . It only remains to give a few figures, in order to afford the reader an idea of the present magnitude of the institution, and the success with which it has met under the able management of Mr. Barnard and Messrs. Dietz & Nelson. The number of miles traveled during the present year is

A B.X. stagecoach at Clinton about 1900. In half a century of service the red and yellow stages transported tens of millions of dollars worth of gold with remarkably few robberies.

110,600. Number of men employed, exclusive of agents whose time is not entirely devoted to the Express, 38. Number of horses employed in the Express service, 160. Number of Expresses despatched from the head office in New Westminster during the present year, 450. Total amount of treasure and valuables, exclusive of merchandise, passing through the Express during the present year, $4,619,000.''

In all, the stagecoaches carried tens of millions of dollars worth of gold from the Cariboo creeks to Yale and Ashcroft. At first a mounted B.C. policeman rode with the stage as escort during the months when the heaviest gold shipments were made, but after several years the service was discontinued because it was considered an unnecessary expense. After that the drivers were on their own. There were remarkably few robbery attempts and only one could be considered a success, although as the robber later peered through prison bars he must have wondered just how successful it was.

One would-be robber was foiled because the driver, Charles Westoby, was deaf. As the story goes, on one trip his six-horse team bolted. Charles, thinking that they were running away for no good reason, grabbed his whip. As he plied the whip he howled in rage: ''I'll teach these sonsabitches to run away!''

When Charles got to the bottom of a mile-long grade, the blown and sweating cayuses settled to a canter. ''That'll teach 'em,'' yelled Charles to his companion, unaware that the man beside him had been trying to explain why the horses had stampeded. Charles hadn't seen a masked man spur his horse out of a gully and try to intercept the stage.

The road agent's warning shot caused the runaway and Charles hadn't heard it. His disability on this occasion, however, earned him a handsome cheque.

On June 25, 1894, a robber named ''Red Bluff'' Charlie had better luck — but not much — when he held up the stagecoach at 150 Mile House and escaped with $45. He was captured next day. On July 4 he faced Judge Clement F. Cornwall and was promptly sentenced to ten years.

Although the bandit didn't realize it, he was lucky to be alive. The driver of the stagecoach he held up was Ed Owens, a quiet man who always carried a six-gun in the waistband of his trousers. He was a deadly shot, demonstrating his ability to passengers by knocking over grouse as the stage rolled along. During the holdup the bandit ordered Owens to get the gold-safe which he did, at the same time planning to draw his revolver and kill the robber. A passenger, however, afraid of being hurt if shooting started put a restraining hand on him. Owens hestitated, then decided to let the bandit live.

A duo which proved to be a man and a woman pulled the last holdup of His Majesty's Mail coach on November 1, 1909, some 8 miles (13 km) south of 150 Mile House. They also had the tough luck to run into Charles Westoby. The result was described by Willis J. West, then general manager of the B.X. Company, in Heritage House book *Stagecoach and Sternwheel Days in the Cariboo and Central B.C.:*

''The regular stage with a full load of passengers left the 150 Mile House early that morning. It was still dark when the stage approached a point

Chief Constable Fred Hussey, inset, and Ashcroft in the time of Rowland's robbery.
A saloon in Ashcroft, perhaps the one patronized by the suddenly wealthy Rowland.

on the road where there was a big tree on one side and a big boulder directly opposite. The woman, dressed like a man, waited behind the tree and the man behind the boulder. When the stage reached them, they both stepped out and covered the driver with their rifles. The man then demanded all the registered mail sacks from 150 Mile House and points north.

"Charles Westoby, the driver, who was quiet deaf, pretended he could not understand their instructions. In the confusion he managed to keep back some of the registered sacks and substitute 'empties' that were being returned to the railway. No attempt was made to rob or molest the passengers. Westoby was ordered to drive on and the stage made good time to the 134 Mile House, the nearest telegraph office. Here word was sent to all telegraph stations up and down the road notifying the police.

"A posse was formed of B.X. employees and ranchers and proceeded to the scene of the hold-up. The police had already arrived to discover that the bandits had taken the mail-sacks a short distance into the brush, coolly cut them open, taken any currency from the letters, but left bank cheques and money-orders. The posse and the police tracked the bandits' barefooted horses for some miles until they encountered the tracks of a band of wild horses, obliging them to turn back and abandon the pursuit.

"The country around 150 Mile House was at that time very sparsely settled. By careful checking and a process of elimination the authorities finally decided that the culprits were a woman and a man whom she called her brother-in-law who had been in the district only a few weeks. The pair were arrested and their cabin searched but the only evidence found was two

freshly shod saddle-horses. After consultations with police headquarters in Victoria, the prisoners were brought down to Ashcroft, put on the train and told to get out and stay out of Canada. They were undoubtedly guilty and were obviously relieved to get off so lightly. It was estimated that they got only about $2,000. They missed one package of $5,000 in currency from the bank in Quesnel owing to driver Westoby's initiative in withholding some of the registered sacks.''

The bandit who put the most original thought into his robbery was Martin Van Buren Rowland, a small barrel-chested man with a black beard. He was lucky enough to select a stage that didn't have Westoby as driver, although he perhaps would have been better off if he had. Rowland's problem turned out to be Frederick S. Hussey, a powerfully-built policeman who rose from the ranks to head the force. In 1891 he was in charge of the vast Kamloops region with the rank of Chief Constable.

It was hot in the Interior that summer, and by mid-August cattlemen were declaring it was the driest spell in fifty years. Stage driver Steve Tingley, southbound to Ashcroft, was also feeling the heat. He reined in his six horses at Bridge Creek near 100 Mile House to give them a breather before tackling the hill ahead. As he reached for a chew of "Mail Pouch" he was surprised by a rather peremptory order: "Stick up your hands!"

As Steve wrapped his reins around the brake handle, then reached skyward, he glimpsed by a roadside stump the gleaming barrel of a Winchester, and behind it the crouching figure of a man.

Slowly the bandit emerged from his ambush, a five-gallon hat shading his eyes, a red bandana over the lower part of his face. He was on the small side and rather thickset.

"All right," he drawled from behind the mask, "throw down the box."

"Ain't got no box," said Steve perfunctorily, matching the utterance with an equally casual squirt of tobacco juice, his hands still shoulder high.

The eyes between the hat brim and the red bandana assumed a rather steely look.

"Throw down that box or I'll blow your head off!" came the rougher command.

There was just enough authority in the tone to help Tingley make up his mind. So the small iron-bound box containing a shipment of gold dust was heaved to the ground.

When news of the robbery reached Ashcroft the alarm went out swiftly. The two Constables at 150 Mile House, Bill Parker and Fred Rose, immediately started scouting the plateau trails for sign of the lone bandit. At the same time, the Constables at Quesnel and Barkerville were alerted.

Constable Joe Burr at Ashcroft set out with a posse and found the strong box, minus its $5-6,000 in gold. But as the days lengthened into weeks with no further lead it seemed as though the undersized bandit had vanished.

Two months later word came of a fabulously rich new gold strike on Scotty Creek which runs into the Bonaparte River between Ashcroft and Clinton. It appeared that a man called Rowland had hit the golden jackpot. Men who still had memories of the Cariboo gold rush made hasty plans to stampede to the new find. Rowland, meanwhile, casually hung around Ashcroft, standing rounds of drinks for his well wishers. Apparently he was on his way to Vancouver to interest some mining men in what promised to be one of the richest strikes in Cariboo history.

While all this was going on Chief Constable Hussey walked into the police office at Ashcroft late one afternoon to see if Burr had picked up anything further on the Bridge Creek robbery.

In time the conversation turned to Rowland and his gold strike. "You think he's really struck something?" said Hussey.

"Looks like it," said Burr, "and it must be pretty rich, the way he's spending around town."

Hussey went over to the window to stare into the street. Something nagged at his mind. For one thing, he remembered hearing that the Chinese had pulled out of Scotty Creek a year ago. After every big clean-up, the last to leave were the Chinese who panned the stream for bare day wages. When the Chinese left, it was a sure sign that nothing of value remained.

There was something else wrong. A man who makes a strike doesn't usually come out and tell the world about it. Not right away, that is. Still another point was vaguely disturbing. The man who held up the stage at Bridge Creek was small and thickset — so was Rowland.

"When did you say Rowland was leaving town?" remarked Hussey, as he turned from the window.

"From what he said he was leaving tonight," said Burr, "on the midnight train."

"Do you know where he left his gold for safe keeping?"

"I did hear he left it at Foster's store," said Joe.

Hussey looked at his watch. It was nine o'clock. With an impatient gesture the Police Chief picked up his hat and shot a quick command at Burr.

"Come on, Joe. Let's find the magistrate and get a warrant for Rowland for that stage robbery."

"But, Chief," Joe protested, "we haven't got any evidence."

Hussey cut him short. A half hour later, with a warrant in his pocket and a rather confused Joe Burr at his side, the Police Chief was heading for Rowland's hotel room.

The little bearded miner was asleep on his bed when they entered.

"Me rob a stage?" he said, when he was fully awake. "You must be out of your mind."

"Maybe," said Hussey, as he ran his hand under the blankets, then the mattress, then the pillow. He touched something hard, something that turned out to be a loaded .45 revolver.

The trio headed for the police station, on their way stopping at Foster's store.

"Mr. Rowland would like the leather bag he left here for safe keeping," said Hussey, then took possession of it.

At the police station Rowland's manner changed. He wanted to make a statement, a written statement.

Hussey obligingly supplied him with pen and paper. For the best part of an hour Rowland wrote the story of his mining career that ended with the Scotty Creek bonanza. When he finished he handed the pages to Hussey who witnessed his signature. Then Joe Burr took him off to a cell.

By the light of an office oil lamp Hussey scanned Rowland's story, Burr waiting for him to finish. When the Police Chief got to the last page, he said, with a smile of satisfaction: "This fellow doesn't know the first thing about mining. He proved it when he wrote this.

"Now bring that lamp over here," he went on, "and let's have that bag of Rowland's gold."

As the golden grains sprinkled over the table, Hussey produced a magnifying glass from his pocket and studied them carefully. He knew that each creek puts its own imprint on the gold it yields — in a way a form of natural finger printing — and veteran miners can tell whether a poke of gold came from one creek or several.

"Just as I thought," he remarked, as he straightened from his task. "This is gold from different creeks. This stuff came out of that strong box on the stage!"

That fall the man who had struck it rich on Scotty Creek was tried at the Clinton Assize. Steve Tingley recognized Rowland's voice and so did some of the passengers. But the clincher was the gold, and a jury of veteran Cariboo prospectors noted the evidence that the gold came from more than one source. They brought in a verdict of "guilty."

Martin Van Buren Rowland got five years.

Lynch Party – Your Country or Mine?

In contrast to the U.S. where during the frontier era lynching was common, B.C.'s history is free from this form of citizens' "justice" — or is it?

Has there ever been a lynching in B.C.? Well, yes and no! There are three recorded instances of citizens becoming the judge, jury and executioner. The first instance probably didn't happen; the second did but a B.C. foursome completed their homespun justice in the U.S.; and in the third a U.S. vigilante committee misjudged the location of the border and strung up their victim in B.C.

The doubtful case is the one reported by English writer and traveller

R. Byron Johnson in his book *Very Far West, Indeed*, published in the early 1860s. According to Johnson, he was partnered with a miner called Jake Walker working a claim at Jack of Clubs Creek near Barkerville. Came fall, and like many others, Johnson wintered in Victoria. When he returned to Barkerville in the spring, Walker told him the story of the lynching.

It seems that after Johnson had left, Walker decided to take advantage of mild weather to get further work done, so he went to Barkerville and hired a helper. A few days later when Walker was down the vertical mine shaft, the helper was up top cranking the windlass when his mind turned to robbery. The primitive apparatus that brought up the ore ran from top to bottom of the shaft and consisted of a broad leather belt with buckets on it. That afternoon the helper quit cranking to peer over the hole and bid Walker goodbye. Then he walked over to the mine shack, stole some food and a few ounces of gold and disappeared.

With the belt and the buckets running free, Walker had to find a way

Victoria's Bastion Square Jail in the 1860s. Here eight men were hanged —legally— and Charlie Brown lost an ear but gained the nickname "One Ear."

of getting out of the hole. If he used his pick to help him climb the shaft walls he had a vision of striking a soft spot and falling to the bottom. If he was injured he might lie there until starvation ended his days.

Then came a sudden inspiration — he drove the pick through the belting and into a timber to anchor the moveable staircase. Then gently he climbed from bucket to bucket to reach the top. When he regained the open air he found he'd been cleaned out of food and his small store of gold.

First he thought of loading up old Betsy and pursuing the robber, then a quasi-legal solution occurred to him. He went in to Barkerville and told his story to a group of miners. From their ranks a posse was formed. They caught up with the delinquent, took him back to Jack of Clubs Creek, read him a short verse or two out of the Bible, then strung him up on a tree. For proof of this Walker took Johnson over to a spot near the creek and showed him a wooden marker over a fresh grave. It bore the date: Dec. 21, 1862.

Early day Victorians dismissed the yarn when the story was published, the chief critic being *Colonist* editor D. W. Higgins. One reason was that Johnson's writing wasn't too accurate, being a hypercritical account of B.C., its resources and its inhabitants. Another reason was that there was no need for a lynching bee around gold-rush Barkerville. The frustrated Walker could very well have told his story to the B.C. Police. The post at Richfield was manned by men who had frequently proved themselves ready, willing and able to pursue and prosecute lawbreakers. There was also a judge called Begbie, not to speak of a jury of Cariboo miners. Apart from Johnson's story there is no other record of this incident. Had it happened, word would have reached the columns of Victoria or New Westminster papers, since anything that happened in the goldfields was given prominence in the papers. Also there would have been mention of it by the police and certainly by Judge Matthew Baillie Begbie.

In the second instance, which occurred during the early 1860s, there is ample documentation in police records and newspaper files. It involved Charlie "One Ear" Brown, a conscienceless scoundrel who landed in Victoria with the mining rush of 1858 and whose life — and death — were well recorded. Instead of heading for the Fraser and fortune. Charlie hung around Victoria peddling whisky to Indians. It was he, and such characters as "Hospital" Hall, "Sebastopol" Jones and others who can be mainly credited with the destruction of the local Songhees band.

Although his product was called whisky, in reality it was straight alcohol. And there was no difficulty in getting it because one pioneer Yates Street druggist advertised 2,000 gallons for sale. This was the era when bootleggers in the American southwest dropped a snake head in the barrel to add "fangs" to the drink. Island bootleggers, by contrast, gave their stock special bouquet by adding camphene, a distillation of oil of turpentine used for illuminating purposes. The resultant blend could light up a whole village!

Time and again Charlie Brown was picked up by the Victoria police, but always went back to whisky peddling. His first conviction was in November 1859. After a spell in the chain gang he was back in again, this time for swindling an Indian out of $20. He said he would deliver whisky, but didn't show up. The record of Brown's brushes with the local law shows that policing in pioneer Victoria was very efficient, despite the undermanned force.

In January 1861, the record shows, Brown was again arrested, this time in his house at the corner of Humboldt and Government for selling a can of alcohol to an Indian woman. (While a "can" may sound innocuous, it contained ten gallons.) This episode netted Charlie a fine or three months on the chain gang. Charlie's finances were obviously low for he chose the chain gang. But he didn't repent. Shortly after his release he was spotted one morning by city police Sergeant George Blake and Superintendent Horace Smith riding on a wagon with a carter called John Guest. They seemed to be heading for a back trail into the Songhees Reserve. They had something in the wagon that interested Smith, so he and Black slipped across the harbor in a boat to cut through the bush and came upon Brown unloading cans of alcohol to four Indians. They watched as he got paid, then as the wagon drove off Smith leaped on to it. Brown and Guest landed in jail.

Meantime back on the reserve, Sergeant Blake was having a brisk time with the Indians who were doing their best to beat out his brains with rocks and clubs. The indomitable Blake, however, clubbed one of them senseless with the butt of his gun. The rest fled and Blake, the Indian and the alcohol came back to the barracks. The Sergeant's day, however, wasn't quite over. While he was locking up the Indian, a Haida brave armed with a loaded revolver dashed past a policeman at the entrance and tried to shoot Blake. Blake, according to his terse report "knocked him down and locked him up, too." For this escapade Brown was fined $500, Guest got off with $100.

A couple of months later Brown was back in again and while awaiting trial met up with an old customer in the jail yard. He was a Haida Indian called "Captain Jefferson" who made a dash for Brown as soon as he saw him. There was a fight, and after they were separated Jefferson made it known that Brown was the man who'd come into the bay one afternoon in the schooner *Laurel* and sold them alcohol — which turned out to be seawater!

There was another fine for Brown, and a week later he and Hospital Hall were back in custody. It was the same story — liquor and Indians. Brown got another $500 fine or one year. The constant arrests had obviously interfered with his source of revenue since he took the year in jail. But he refused to work and was locked in his cell at the grim Bastion Street Jail, his food bread and water. Here occurred an incident that for Brown would have disastrous consequences.

One afternoon jailer Charles B. Wright had to move Brown from one cell to another. When he entered the whisky peddler's cell, Brown backed up against the wall with the warning: "You. . . . If you lay a hand on me, I'll murder you."

In the ensuing struggle, Brown got a headlock on the jailer, but Wright managed to draw his gun and put the muzzle alongside Charlie's ear with the admonition: "Let go, or I'll blow your head off."

When Brown ignored the warning, Wright pulled the trigger. Charlie lost an ear but gained a nickname, "One Ear." In addition, at the November

In the early 1860s Charlie "One Ear" Brown was a criminal well known to the police forces of both New Westminster, above, and Victoria. In Victoria, for instance, he was sentenced to the chain gang which tamped into city streets rocks like those shown below.

Assize he came up before Judge Cameron charged with assaulting a peace officer. He got another year.

About this time, news of the Cariboo gold rush struck Victoria like a fever, causing hundreds to dash northward. Bootlegger Brown also heard the news as, fettered in irons, he tamped rocks on a downtown street. Feigning illness, he got into hospital, and a few days later escaped. "If he has left the Island," said the local police, "it's good riddance."

After a two-year series of lawless escapades on the Mainland, Brown was back in Victoria and in court again, this time for stealing a boat. He jumped his bail and a warrant was issued. It was now 1863, and word had trickled in from far off Wild Horse Creek in the East Kootenay of another phenomenal gold discovery. "Bigger than Cariboo" flashed the word.

Even though Wild Horse was over 400 wilderness miles (645 km) east of the Fraser River across several mountain ranges, by 1864 the rush was on. The creek was quickly covered with acres of tents housing between 5,000 and 6,000 men, the tents in turn giving way to the shanty town of Fisherville. Excited miners found themselves digging $40,000 to $60,000 a week out of the ground, and in a few months Fisherville was a second Barkerville. It was a mad scene, where one miner took $30,000 out of a hundred square feet of ground, another picked out of his shovel a 36-ounce nugget worth $700. So crazy did the tempo become that in 1866 the miners dismantled the whole town of Fisherville to get at the gold beneath the buildings.

While there were wild characters among Fisherville's residents — men like "Dancing Bill" Latham, "Black Jack" Smyth and "Yeast Powder" Bill Denniston — they were all relatively law abiding. Assurance that this condition would continue arrived in the guise of Gold Commissioner J. C. Haynes and a single policeman, William Young. So isolated was the region that they had been twenty days in the saddle from Osoyoos in the Okanagan Valley.

Haynes immediately assumed his official duties since the miners had "Yeast Powder" in custody awaiting the arrival of the law. Seems that there were two factions in the mining camp: U.S. miners and Canadian miners, the latter in the minority. On August 9, the two groups met in front of the Fortier Cafe where a vocal young Irishman, Thomas Walker who was the leader of the Canadian faction, got into an argument with Yeast Powder Bill and pulled his revolver. Unfortunately for him he only succeeded in shooting the end of Yeast Powder's thumb. With his good hand Yeast Powder pulled one of his two guns and shot Walker through the heart.

"Overland" Bob Evans then started shooting and a free-for-all ensued. When the fracas ended casualties included Overland Bob so badly wounded that he was three months recovering, a man named Kelly stabbed in the back, and another called Paddy Skie clubbed so hard that he was unconscious for months.

An account of subsequent events was written by D. M. Drumheller in his book, *"Uncle Dan" Drumheller Tells Thrills of Western Trails.* . . . "A mob was quickly raised by the friends of Tommy Walker for the purpose of hanging Overland Bob and Yeast Powder Bill. Then a law and order organization numbering about 1,000 miners, of which I was a member, assembled. It was the purpose of our organization to order a miners' court

In 1864 a Constable and Judge Haynes, left, were twenty days on horseback travelling from the Okanagan to Wild Horse Creek. They promptly established law and order, although by then Thomas Walker had been killed in a shoot-out. His grave is still preserved by public-spirited citizens of the East Kootenay.

and give all concerned a fair trial. Our organization took care of the . . . wounded men and put a strong guard around them. The next morning we appointed a lawyer by the name of A. J. Gregory as trial judge and John McClellan sheriff, with authority to appoint as many deputies as he wished. That was the condition of things when Judge Haines (Haynes), the British Columbia Commissioner, rode into camp.

" 'Fifteen hundred men under arms in the queen's dominion. A dastardly usurpation of authority, don't cher know,' remarked Judge Haines. But one little English constable with knee breeches, red cap, cane in his hand, riding a jockey saddle and mounted on a bob-tailed horse, quelled that mob in 15 minutes."

Haynes relieved the "sheriff" of further duties and held an inquest. Although the jury was confused about who shot whom in the gun duel, they felt that Yeast Powder Bill had acted in self defence. A subsequent preliminary hearing agreed and Yeast Powder Bill was set free.

To prevent a reoccurrence, Haynes decreed that revolvers were to be kept at home. The consequence was impressive. A short time later when Colonial Secretary Arthur N. Birch reached Wild Horse after twenty-four days on horseback from the Fraser River, he reported: "I found the British Columbia mining laws in full force, all customs duties paid, no pistols to be seen and everything as quiet and orderly as it could possibly be in the most civilized district of the colony."

The presence of a judge and, later, three additional policemen — Jack Lawson, James Normansell and John Carrington — ensured that conditions there would remain "quiet and orderly." The law took hold in quiet but effective style. On one occasion Carrington escorted a prisoner over 500 miles (805 km) to New Westminster, all but the last 100 miles (160 km) on horseback. The prisoner's crime? Not paying duty on a ham.

Although Jack Lawson was a rookie he was soon popular with the roughshod community. The depth of this popularity and the respect the miners had for the policemen was soon demonstrated — and it involved Charlie "One Ear" Brown.

Brown, having decided that both Victoria and New Westminster chain gangs weren't to his liking, moved over the border. One day in the spring of 1867 he arrived at Kootenay Trading Post a few miles south of the B.C. border.

True to character, he stole two horses from a rancher's corral and headed for Wild Horse Creek, camping one night about 4 miles (6.4 km) from Fisherville, or what was left of it. The owners of the horses, two Dutchmen, followed his trail until they found and reconnoitered his camp. They then went into Wild Horse to tell the police.

All the police were on patrol except Lawson who heard their story and good naturedly offered to get their horses back. Next morning the trio swung into the saddle and rode to Brown's camp. After an hour's ride Lawson, who was in the lead, spotted Brown coming down a trail. The Constable stopped him and as he asked about the horses, he noticed Brown's hand slipping toward the inside of his jacket. Drawing his gun, Lawson gave the outlaw curt instruction to keep his hands in the air, but turned his head for an instant to beckon the Dutchmen forward. It was a split-second error that cost Lawson his life. With a lightning draw Brown put a pistol bullet through the back of Lawson's head. The unfortunate officer reeled in the saddle and fell to the ground. The two ranchers put spurs to their horses and disappeared. Brown dismounted, took the policeman's gun, and left.

The excited Dutchmen galloped into Wild Horse and told their tragic story to a group of grim and silent miners. Four of the listeners, with cryptic nods and interjections, readied their horses, found arms and ammunition, and left in search of Charlie Brown.

In a relentless feat of tracking they found where the fugitive had crossed St. Mary's River on a raft, losing most of his supplies in the rough water. Next they came to Joe Davis' camp where they found the lop-eared bandit had got food and continued on a mountain trail. Some 12 miles (19 km) from Davis' camp they met a Chinese. Yes, he'd seen a man with a missing ear; he wanted ammunition but the Chinese didn't have any. On they went, next checking with a blacksmith who said the earless fugitive got food from him. Brown was well armed and boastful, recounting how he had killed a B.C. policeman and how he was going to shoot a couple of Dutchmen at the first opportunity.

It wasn't long after that the avenging quartet crossed the border into the U.S., their horses raising clouds of white alkali dust as they neared Bonner's Ferry. There they met an Indian who had just been accosted by a lone horseman, a one-eared man. He wanted ammunition. The miners were nearing the end of their quest. The *British Columbian* newspaper at New Westminster carried the sequel:

"Leaving their jaded horses at the Ferry, and disguising themselves with moccasins, and etc., they pushed forward until hearing of his having crossed the Kootenay and struck the trail at the head of the lake, they lay in wait for him. Seeing no footprints of either man or beast on the trail, Brown pressed on, thinking himself safe. They soon saw him advancing at a rapid pace, with the remaining pistol in one hand and a knife in the other. Three of them raised their guns, double barreled guns, loaded with buckshot and fired simultaneously, literally riddling his dastardly carcass. Returning on the following day, they dug a hole into which they put the remains of Charles Brown, the thief and cowardly murderer. He lies close by the side of the Walla Walla trail, 43 miles south of the boundary line. Brown figured at Victoria, at Hope, Sumass and other places some years ago, and bore a character far from good."

Brown's unlamented departure wasn't exactly a B.C. lynching in the true sense of the word. But it would have been if the Wild Horse miners had caught up with One Ear in B.C.

Seventeen years later, however, there was a lynching in B.C. It occurred in the Fraser Valley community of Huntingdon which adjoins Sumas, Washington, and was the reverse of the One Ear Brown episode.

On February 26, 1884, Louie (Mesatchie) Sam, a Chilliwack Indian, went across the boundary to Sumas and into the store of Joe Bell at Nooksack Crossing. There was felony in Louie's heart, for he held a gun on Bell and demanded money. Joe Bell demurred and a bullet from the Indian's gun ended his days. Louie fled back to Canada. When word of the episode reached Huntingdon, two or three residents grabbed the murderer and confined him in the house of a farmer, Fraser York.

With their ingrained respect for law and order these British Columbians were going to take Louie to New Westminster next morning and hand him over to the law. Fate decided otherwise. In the evening gloom a crowd of men from across the border, bearing lanterns and rifles, crowded on York's porch and demanded the Indian. Whether the Indian was handed over, or whether the Sumas committee broke down York's door and took him by force, is immaterial. What was clear was that they were going to take him back across the border and hang him.

Next morning some Huntingdon residents found Louie swinging from the limb of a tree just 168 paces north of the boundary line. Whether the Sumas group mistook their bearings in the dark and thought they were in Washington is a matter for conjecture. Anyway, the incident is the only authentic lynching to take place in B.C. — by 168 paces.

In Memorium

On May 6, 1865, John D.B. Ogilvie became the first lawman murdered in British Columbia.

It was May 6, 1865, and near the community of Bella Coola on the B.C. coast the 80-ton trading schooner *Langley* swung at anchor in a little bay. Forward in the ship's fo'c'sle an oil lamp swinging in a gimbal cast eerie shadows as skipper Smith poked some wood in the stove preparatory to making coffee. Nearby, on a locker, sat big, bearded B.C. Police Constable J. D. B. "Jack" Ogilvie, sole representative of the law between Cape Caution and the Skeena River — 200 miles (320 km) as the crow flies but several thousand along the fjords which characterize the region.

As the men talked, they didn't notice the door of the forward chain locker slowly open. From it peered an evil-looking face, unshaven with eyes deep set and treacherous. The man behind the face — 35-year-old French-Canadian Antoine Lucanage — raised a heavy Colt revolver, levelled it at the unsuspecting police officer and pulled the trigger.

The crashing report rocked the little cabin. In an acrid, billowing cloud of black-powder smoke Ogilvie got slowly to his feet then slumped down. Skipper Smith, with one quick glance at the gunman's hideout, fled up the companionway to the deck. There he found Morris Moss, a coastal fur trader and Ogilvie's friend.

A few days earlier Ogilvie had asked Moss to help him capture some renegade whites who were selling liquor to the Indians. Chief of them was Antoine Lucanage who on April 1, 1865, in broad daylight boldly sailed right into Bella Coola. He and his boat were seized by Ogilvie and Lucanage was shipped to jail at New Westminster on a passing schooner.

On the way he jumped overboard at the south end of Johnstone Strait and despite swirling tide rips miraculously reached shore. He was later picked up by the *Langley* whose skipper was unaware that Lucanage was on his way to jail. By a strange quirk of fate Bella Coola was among her stopping places. At Bella Coola Lucanage slipped ashore at night. When Ogilvie heard of the incident he mustered some Indians and searched the area but found no trace of the fugitive.

A couple of days later when the *Langley* left, Ogilvie had a hunch that

Lucanage had somehow regained the vessel. "Let's catch her up and search her," was his quick suggestion to Moss.

With six swiftly paddling Indians the pair set off and about four hours later caught the schooner. Her skipper Smith swore that the fugitive wasn't aboard. Ten minutes later came the dramatic moment when Lucanage fired the shot from the chain locker.

Smith rushed up on deck to incoherently tell his story to Moss, who promptly grabbed a lantern to go down in the fo'c'sle after the gunman. At that moment, however, Ogilvie staggered up on deck. Then Lucanage appeared, knife in one hand, revolver in the other.

Constable Ogilvie, though mortally wounded, grappled with the cutthroat and wrested the gun from him. Then, as Lucanage turned and ran towards a companionway, Ogilvie fired two shots at him. Moss, aft at the wheel, drew his revolver and ran forward but the mainsail boom swung over and hurled him into the water. The Indians in the canoe heard him yell and picked him up.

When Moss got back on board he noticed that Ogilvie was near total collapse. He and Smith packed the wounded man below, and as they were doing so Lucanage escaped in a skiff. Below deck, Ogilvie lived only a few more minutes.

The murder stirred the Colony and the government offered a $1,000 reward for Lucanage's capture. Despite the reward and a protracted search he was never found alive, although he was variously reported as far south as San Francisco. Finally, several months later a corpse was found on northern Vancouver Island and identified as Lucanage. How he died remains a mystery and the reward, probably the equivalent of some $75,000 today, was never claimed.

OTHER POLICEMEN WHO DIED ON DUTY

Constable John Lawson, Wildhorse Creek, April 1867

Constable John T. Ussher, Kamloops, December 1879

Constable Geoffrey H. Aston, Okanagan Lake, March 1912

Constable Alexander Kindness, Clinton, May 1912

Constable Henry Westaway, Union Bay, March 1913

Constable George Stanfield, Grand Forks, June 1920

Constable Arthur W. Mable, Kamloops, September 1926

Constable Percival Carr, Merritt, May 1934

Inspector Wm. J. Service, Prince Rupert, July 1938

Sergeant Robert Gibson, Prince Rupert, July 1938

Constable Clifford A. Prescott, Princess Royal Island, June 1939

Constable Frank Clark, Victoria, November 1941

A selection of other HERITAGE HOUSE titles:

The PIONEER DAYS IN BRITISH COLUMBIA Series

Every article is true, many written or narrated by those who, 100 or more years ago, lived the experiences they relate. Each volume contains 160 pages in large format magazine size (8½ x 11), four-color covers, some 60,000 words of text and over 200 historical photos, many published for the first time.

A continuing Canadian best seller in three volumes which have sold over 75,000 copies. Each volume, $12.95

WHITE SLAVES OF THE NOOTKA

On March 22, 1803, while anchored in Nootka Sound on the West Coast of Vancouver Island, the *Boston* was attacked by "friendly" Nootka Indians. Twenty-five of her 27 crew were massacred, their heads "arranged in a line" for survivor John Jewitt to identify. Jewitt and another survivor became 2 of 50 slaves owned by Chief Maquina, never knowing what would come first — rescue or death.

The account of their ordeal, published in 1815, remains remarkably popular. New Western Canadian edition, well illustrated. 128 pages. $9.95

THE DEATH OF ALBERT JOHNSON: Mad Trapper of Rat River

Albert Johnson in 1932 triggered the greatest manhunt in Canada's Arctic history. In blizzards and numbing cold he was involved in four shoot-outs, killing one policeman and gravely wounding two other men before being shot to death.

This revised, enlarged edition includes photos taken by "Wop" May, the legendary bush pilot whose flying skill saved two lives during the manhunt. Another Canadian best seller. $7.95

OUTLAWS AND LAWMEN OF WESTERN CANADA

These true police cases prove that our history was anything but dull. Chapters in 160-page Volume Three, for instance, include Saskatchewan's Midnight Massacre, The Yukon's Christmas Day Assassins, When Guns Blazed at Banff, and Boone Helm — The Murdering Cannibal.

Each of the three volumes in this Canadian best seller series is well illustrated with maps and photos, with four-color photos on the covers. Volume One, $8.95; Volume Two, $8.95; Volume Three, $9.95

B.C. PROVINCIAL POLICE STORIES: Mystery and Murder from the Files of Western Canada's First Lawmen

The B.C. Police, born in 1858, were the first lawmen in Western Canada. During their 90 years of service they established a reputation as one of the most progressive police forces in North America. All cases in these best selling titles are reconstructed from archives and police files.

Volume One: 16 chapters, many photos, 128 pages. $9.95
Volume Two: 22 chapters, many photos, 144 pages. $9.95
Volume Three: 23 chapters, many photos, 160 pages. $12.95

B.C. BACKROADS

This best selling series contains complete information from Vancouver through the Fraser Canyon to Cache Creek, east to Kamloops country and north to the Cariboo. Also from Vancouver to Bridge River-Lillooet via Whistler. Each book contains mile-by-mile route mileage, history, fishing holes, wildlife, maps and photos.

Volume One — Garibaldi to Bridge River Country-Lillooet. $9.95
Volume Three — Junction Country: Boston Bar to Clinton. $9.95
Thompson-Cariboo: Highways, byways, backroads. $4.95

An Explorer's Guide: MARINE PARKS OF B.C.

To tens of thousands of boaters, B.C.'s Marine Parks are as welcome and convenient as their popular highway equivalents. This guide includes anchorages and onshore facilities, trails, picnic areas, campsites, history and other information. In addition, it is profusely illustrated with color and black and white photos, maps and charts.

Informative reading for boat owners from runabouts to cabin cruisers. 200 pages $12.95.

GO FISHING WITH THESE BEST SELLING TITLES

HOW TO CATCH SALMON — BASIC FUNDAMENTALS

The most popular salmon book ever written. Information on trolling, rigging tackle, most productive lures, proper depths, salmon habits, downriggers, where to find fish, and much more.

Sales over 130,000. 176 pages. $5.95

HOW TO CATCH SALMON — ADVANCED TECHNIQUES

The most comprehensive advanced salmon fishing book available. Over 200 pages crammed full of how-to-tips and easy-to-follow diagrams. Covers all popular salmon fishing methods: mooching, trolling with bait, spoons and plugs, catching giant chinook, and a creel full of other information.

A continuing best seller. 192 pages. $11.95

HOW TO CATCH CRABS: How popular is this book? This is the 11th printing, with sales over 90,000. $4.95

HOW TO CATCH BOTTOMFISH: Revised and expanded. $5.95

HOW TO CATCH SHELLFISH: Updated 4th printing. 144 pages. $3.95

HOW TO CATCH TROUT by Lee Straight, one of Canada's top outdoorsmen. 144 pages. $5.95

HOW TO COOK YOUR CATCH: Cooking seafood on the boat, in a camper or at the cabin. 8th printing. 192 pages. $4.95

FLY FISH THE TROUT LAKES

with Jack Shaw

Professional outdoor writers describe the author as a man "who can come away regularly with a string when everyone else has been skunked." In this book, he shares over 40 years of studying, raising and photographing all forms of lake insects and the behaviour of fish to them.

Written in an easy-to-follow style. 96 pages. $8.95

SALMON FISHING BRITISH COLUMBIA: Volumes One and Two

Since B.C. has some 7,000 miles of coastline, a problem to its 400,000 salmon anglers is where to fish. These books offer a solution. Volume One includes over 100 popular fishing holes around Vancouver Island. Volume Two covers the Mainland Coast from Vancouver to Jervis Inlet. Both include maps, gear to use, best times, lures and a tackle box full of other information.

Volume One — Vancouver Island. $9.95
Volume Two — Mainland Coast: Vancouver to Jervis Inlet. $11.95
